# Howards End
# is on the
# Landing

## BOOKS BY SUSAN HILL INCLUDE

Novels
*I'm the King of the Castle* (Somerset Maugham Award)
*Strange Meeting*
*In the Springtime of the Year*
*The Bird of Night* (Whitbread Award, Booker Prize shortlisted)
*Air and Angels*
*The Woman in Black*
*The Mist in the Mirror*
*The Man in the Picture*
*The Beacon*

Non-Fiction
*The Magic Apple Tree*
*Family*

Children's Books
*The Glass Angels*
*The Battle for Gullywith*

# Howards End is on the Landing

A YEAR OF READING FROM HOME

Susan Hill

PROFILE BOOKS

'To my friends pictured within.'

First published in Great Britain in 2009 by
PROFILE BOOKS LTD
3A Exmouth House
Pine Street
London EC1R 0JH
*www.profilebooks.com*

1 3 5 7 9 10 8 6 4 2

Typeset in Transitional by MacGuru Ltd
*info@macguru.org.uk*
Printed and bound in Great Britain by
Clays, Bungay, Suffolk

ISBN 978 1 84668 265 0

The paper this book is printed on is certified by the © 1996 Forest Stewardship
Council A.C. (FSC). It is ancient-forest friendly. The printer holds FSC chain of
custody SGS-COC-2061

**FSC**
**Mixed Sources**
Product group from well-managed
forests and other controlled sources
Cert no. SGS-COC-2061
www.fsc.org
© 1996 Forest Stewardship Council

# Starting Point

IT BEGAN LIKE THIS. I went to the shelves on the landing to look for a book I knew was there. It was not. But plenty of others were and among them I noticed at least a dozen I realised I had never read.

I pursued the elusive book through several rooms and did not find it in any of them, but each time I did find at least a dozen, perhaps two dozen, perhaps two hundred, that I had never read.

And then I picked out a book I had read but had forgotten I owned. And another and another. After that came the books I had read, knew I owned and realised that I wanted to read again.

I found the book I was looking for in the end, but by then it had become far more than a book. It marked the start of a journey through my own library.

Some people give up drink for January or chocolate for Lent, others decide to live for a year on just a pound a day, or without buying any new clothes. Their reasons may be financial (to save money), physical (to lose weight), or spiritual (to become more holy). I decided to spend a year reading only books already on my shelves for several reasons.*

The journey through my own books involved giving up buying new ones, and that will seem a perverse act for someone who is both an author and a publisher. But this was a personal journey, not a mission. I felt the need to get to know my own books again, but I am not about to persuade other people to abandon the purchase of new ones.

I wanted to repossess my books, to explore what I had accumulated over a lifetime of reading, and to map this house of many volumes. There are enough here to divert, instruct, entertain, amaze, amuse, edify, improve, enrich me for far longer than a year and every one of them deserves to be taken down and dusted off, opened and read. A book which is left on a shelf is a dead thing but it is also a chrysalis, an inanimate object packed with the potential to burst into new life. Wandering through the house that day looking for one elusive book, my eyes were opened to how much of that life was stored here, neglected or ignored.

The start of the journey also coincided with my decision to curtail my use of the internet, which can have an insidious, corrosive effect. Too much internet usage fragments the brain and dissipates concentration so that after a while, one's ability to spend long, focused hours immersed in a single subject becomes blunted. Information comes pre-digested in small pieces, one grazes on endless ready-meals and snacks of the mind, and the result is mental malnutrition.

---

*(There were one or two caveats. I would borrow academic books from libraries and I would read some of the books sent by literary editors, for review.)

The internet can also have a pernicious influence on reading because it is full of book-related gossip and chatter on which it is fatally easy to waste time that should be spent actually paying close, careful attention to the books themselves, whether writing them or reading them.

Rationing it strictly gave me back more than time. Within a few days, my attention span increased again, my butterfly-brain settled down and I was able to spend longer periods concentrating on single topics, difficult long books, subjects requiring my full focus. It was like diving into a deep, cool ocean after flitting about in the shallows, Slow Reading as against Gobbling-up.

I did not begin my year of reading from home in order to save money, but of course that is what happened. I buy too many books, excusing impulse purchases on the vague grounds that buying a new paperback is better for me than buying a bar of chocolate. But that depends on the quality of the paperback. I wanted to reacquaint myself with old books and resist the pressure to buy something because it was new, because it was in the top twenty or shortlisted for the Booker Prize or even the Nobel, for that matter, or recommended by Richard and Judy or discounted, heavily promoted or chattered about on the internet. A friend joined a book club because she wanted to expand her literary horizons and left it because the only titles ever chosen were the latest hyped or shortlisted novels. There is no doubt that of the thousands of new books published every year many are excellent and some will stand the test of time. A few will become classics. But I wanted to stand back and let the dust settle on everything new, while I set off on a journey through my books.

What follows is a description of that journey, which has also and inevitably led to my thinking, remembering, ordering, assessing, my entire book-reading life. I have let myself recall places where I read, bookshelves of the past, gone back in my imagination to libraries I used to know, and know intimately, libraries I visited daily and which contributed to forming me, changing me, helping me to grow. Books lead to people, of course. Over the past fifty years I have had the privilege of meeting some of the great writers of our time. As a young writer I was very lucky to be introduced to people whose work already meant a great deal to me and many of them gave me help and advice at a stage in my career when it was invaluable. So many taught me a lesson I have tried never to forget – that the young need encouragement. They also need a few allowances made for naivety and bumptiousness. This book is not an autobiography in the usual sense but it is a record of so much more than just reading, more than just books. Name-dropping is a tiresome, if harmless, trait. But I have been encouraged and inspired by many people in the world of books, not all of whose names I remember (or perhaps even knew): librarians, bookshop staff, school and university teachers, fellow readers, correspondents. I salute them, too, for I owe them so much.

The journey began one early autumn afternoon, in the old farm-house where I live, surrounded by the gently rising hills and graceful trees, the ploughed and planted fields, the hedgerows and flower borders and orchards and old stone walls, the deer and birds and hedgehogs and rabbits, the foxes and badgers and moths and bees of Gloucestershire. I climbed two flights of elm-wood stairs to the top landing in search of a book, and found myself embarked on a year of travelling through the books of a lifetime.

# No Order, No Order

I SOMETIMES WONDER if the books came into this house or if the house grew around them. Either way, they feel as organic a part of it as the beams, the Aga in the kitchen, the wood burner in the sitting room, or the old pine wardrobe that arrived in half a dozen sections and had to be assembled once it was in the right bedroom. The bookshelves were built or bought to fit not only whole walls but nooks and crannies and have filled up in the same slightly haphazard way over the years. I can think of only one shelf which was made to measure, for very small books, mainly the Oxford World's Classics series printed on fine paper and published in demy octavo. The old words for book sizes are still in use – Demy, Quarto, Royal – just like the old names for paper sizes, though others go alongside them: B Format, and A2, A3. I hope those of us who learned pints and quarts, feet and inches, pounds and ounces, let alone pecks and bushels, can be forgiven a fondness for the old-fashioned terminology.

Next to the World's Classics on the shelf above the door is a long row of small square Observer Books, which I started to collect as a child, alongside the I Spy series. The Observer books of Moths, Birds' Eggs, Aeroplanes, Trees, Churches, Archaeology, Ferns, Mosses … I sometimes take a handful down and pore over forgotten facts about the Tiger Hawk Moth or the Wild Service Tree, the Saddleback Church and the Spitfire. Someone once told me that these were the sort of books that boys like because they are essentially lists and boys like lists more than girls do. I wonder.

I know people whose books are housed in something resembling public libraries, one or two whose books are even catalogued, in card indexes, on spreadsheets or even on infernal systems on websites where it is possible to log your own library and arrange virtual books on virtual shelves.

I know people who own thousands of books and can tell you the exact spot where every single one of them is shelved. They colour coordinate them, or arrange them by alphabet or author or subject. Well, that is what collectors enjoy doing, with books arranged like stamps in albums. Good luck to them. My father's sock drawer was just the same.

Alas, there is no plan to the housing of the books here, no classification system, no order – or rather, there is an order, one that has come about by a process of accumulation and illogic, and the small but constant shifts and changes in family life, activity and volume-acquisition. It works. Yes, books do go missing. I take one from its place, wander into another room and put it down, leave it on my bedside or the kitchen table. In a rare fit of helpfulness, someone else may even put it back on a shelf, though probably not the one from which it came.

But if I were an orderly person with a Dewey decimal classification system, I would never have gone hunting for the elusive book, reached the second-floor landing, and the start of this journey.

A book collector would be better organised, but I am not a book collector. I have spent my life working with books in numerous ways. I have accumulated a wide assortment of them over sixty-plus years and many, many have gone – lent or left, sold or given away, for there is nothing essentially sacred about a book just because it is printed on paper and bound between covers. Only look at the rubbish available in book form. Some are quickly read, been, gone. You don't read many thrillers twice. Others served a temporary practical need – your cat was having kittens and you needed to know how to look after them; you were travelling to Denmark and wanted a guide. But the kittens grew up and the cat was neutered and you will never visit Denmark again. Pass the thriller to a friend, give the cat book to the charity shop, sell the guide to Denmark on eBay. You don't have to pay its rent just because it is a book.

When I did not find my elusive title upstairs, I came down to the room I call the Small Dark Den. I would not want to spend a year in it, but it has such an eclectic mixture on its shelves that I could probably spend one just reading books taken from it.

It's an odd room and one that, uniquely in this house, gets little natural light – it faces north, and the side of a stone barn, and it's overshadowed by an old walnut tree. No amount of Brilliant White emulsion ever made it lighter so we gave up and lined the walls with bookshelves instead. The SDD also houses the piano which no one now ever plays, and the television on which I watch rubbish.

The Small Dark Den has a long row of dull-looking, uniform books bound in porridge-coloured card with hessian on the spine and titles in black Times Roman. They are old plays published by the Malone Society, they belong to the Shakespeare Professor, and I have never read a single one nor will I, even in this year. But the titles made me take a few down and open them.

*The Wisdom of Dr Dodypoll* (1600)
[Actus Prima. A Curtaine drawne. Earl Lassinbergh is discovered (like a Painter) painting Lucilia, who sits working on a piece of Cushion worke.]
*The Play of the Wether*
(A new and a very merry interlude of all manner wethers made by John Heywood.)
*The Hog Hath Lost his Pearl*
*The Downfall of Robert, Earl of Huntingdon*
*The Faithfull Friends*
*An Interlude called Lusty Juventus*
*The Queen of Corsica*
*The Shepherd's Paradise*
*The Pardoner and the Friar and the Four Ps*

On and on they run and if they were novels I would be reading them, but Elizabethan plays are not as enticing as their titles and if they were any good we would have heard of them, as we have heard of *The Merchant of Venice*, *The Duchess of Malfi* and *Dr Faustus*.

These books are facsimiles, too, and several are printed in old Gothic font which is almost impossible for modern eyes to take in.

Ah, fonts. Typeface. Hot metal. Typography. Printing Presses. We'll be here all night. In the Small Dark Den there is a book called *An Alphabet of Fonts* and sometimes I look through it and gaze at their beauty and the subtle, subtle differences between each one. If you ask me to choose my favourite I would need three – Garamond, Perpetua and one other. But that is hard to find. It was designed by Ralph Beyer for the new Coventry Cathedral, consecrated in 1962, and it is not a font you can order from your printer, but if you go to the Cathedral you will see it everywhere, on the lettering carved on stone, and the Orders of Service. It is strange to have a font, of all things, bound up with your life, but this one speaks to me of places and people and a time, all precious to me; if you cut me open, I daresay that whatever is carved upon my heart will be in Ralph Beyer lettering.

The titles of the old plays reprinted by the Malone Society are in Times Roman, the font everyone recognises, the classic font and one which serves almost every purpose and always looks handsome, though I prefer Garamond. But whatever the font, it must have a serif or I cannot read much of it. There is a long modern novel on one of the shelves of the Small Dark Den that I certainly should read. It came to me with recommendations from all sides, but I can't read it because it is printed in a sans serif font, Arial, probably, and I simply cannot force my eyes to take it in for more than a few lines. Why should that be? Do others agree with me? Do publishers think about these things? This one does.

Publishers also think about titles, but I wonder, with both my author's and my publisher's hats on, if we think about them quite enough. I love book titles and they're important. Many a new novel has sunk without trace because it has a dull, unmemorable title. *One of Us. Two by Two. Far and Near*. I made those up but you could find plenty like them and if you saw them in a shop your eye would slide over them; if someone recommended one you would instantly forget what it was called.

A good title beckons, attracts, seduces, remains. I have plenty of favourite titles though oddly enough they are not necessarily attached to favourite books. A good title makes a pattern, has a rhythm and can be rolled very satisfactorily round in the mouth, even recited like a verse to cheer up dull moments.

*The Heart is a Lonely Hunter*
*The Ballad of the Sad Café*
*The Tenant of Wildfell Hall*
*Salmon Fishing in the Yemen*
*Tinker, Tailor, Soldier, Spy*
*The Mysterious Affair at Styles*
*A Woman's Guide to Adultery*
*All Fun and Games until Somebody Loses an Eye*
*The Curious Incident of the Dog in the Night-Time*
*Agatha Raisin and the Quiche of Death*
*We Need to Talk About Kevin*
*If on a Winter's Night a Traveller …*
*Flaubert's Parrot*
*The Man with the Golden Gun*
*The Scarlet Letter*
*The Hound of the Baskervilles*
*The Prime of Miss Jean Brodie*
*The Earth Hums in B Flat*

They all have a certain ring. They make you want to read the book.

I could have begun my year of reading from home anywhere in the house, anywhere on the shelves. I had no agenda to follow, no lists to tick off, no syllabus or plan to follow.

I began more or less at random by taking down a box of books that was sitting next to the Malone Society Classics in the SDD.

In 1985 Penguin celebrated their fiftieth year by publishing a set of their first ten titles from 1935 in a handsome box. I had two sets, one of which I have left on the shelf untouched and still muffled in its original shrink-wrap. These things are sometimes worth keeping.

I am cynical about anniversaries. Publishers, like the BBC, make a fuss about the tenth or the twenty-fifth or the centenary since they started imprint X or first published author Y or bound in the colour Z but it's often just a pretext for a self-congratulatory party and some re-jacketing – the general public isn't much interested. But I was very aware of the Penguin 1935–85 set because it was issued the year my third daughter was born and my husband gave me one as a present, for reading-while-feeding. I associate the books with sitting up in the middle of the night quietly reading Mary Webb's *Gone to Earth* and Compton Mackenzie's *Carnival* by the soft light of the nursery lamp. (The other titles in the set are André Maurois' *Ariel*, Hemingway's *A Farewell to Arms*, Eric Linklater's *Poet's Pub*, *William* by E.H. Young and Agatha Christie's *The Mysterious Affair at Styles*.)

Now, on a golden day in late September, I took two books out to a deckchair in the garden. The first apples were thumping down. The last swallows were dipping and soaring, dipping and soaring over the pond. A dragonfly hovered, its electric-blue back catching the sunlight. There had been an early mist and cobwebs draped over the long grass like parasols caught and held on their four corners. The air smelled of damp earth.

I opened the first slim paperback, a perfect facsimile with its green jacket and old-fashioned print.

*The Unpleasantness at the Bellona Club* by Dorothy L. Sayers.

'What in the world, Wimsey, are you doing in this Morgue?' demanded Captain Fentiman, flinging aside the *Evening Banner* with the air of a man released from an irksome duty.

'Oh, I wouldn't call it that,' retorted Wimsey amiably. 'Funeral Parlour at the very least. Look at the marble. Look at the furnishings. Look at the palms and the chaste bronze nude in the corner.'

'Yes, and look at the corpses. Place always reminds me of that old thing in *Punch*, you know "Waiter, take away Lord Whatsisname, he's been dead two days."'

The opening lines set the scene, the Bellona Club in London St James's, and a world which I would say no longer exists – except that it does. Walk into the Athenaeum, Whites or Brooks's and you walk back into the world Wimsey knew so well, with the deep, high-backed leather armchairs, the smoking room, heavy curtains at the tall windows, the round mahogany tables set out with newspapers and journals, neatly edge to edge, the slightly hushed voices, and, somewhere offstage, the clink of china and the faint pat of playing cards on green baize. Sayers is one of a clutch of writers belonging to what is always known as the Golden Age of the Detective Story. When did the detective story, beloved of and sometimes written by Oxford and Cambridge dons, metamorphose into the Crime Novel? Probably not until the end of the twentieth century, though in America great novelists and stylists like Raymond Chandler are better described as crime or even thriller-writers than writers of detective stories.

The world of Lord Peter Wimsey is quintessentially English,

1920s and 1930s. And *The Unpleasantness at the Bellona Club* is a classic example. As in the ancient *Punch* joke quoted in the opening lines, the body of General Fentiman is found, apparently asleep but actually dead, in one of those deep armchairs and at first it is assumed that he died of natural causes – old man, bitter weather, dickey heart. But Wimsey is not satisfied that this is the case and sets out, with his sidekick Bunter – a sort of amateur-detective's Jeeves – to unravel the mystery. When the police become involved, it is naturally in the person of Wimsey's friend Inspector Parker, who allows Lord Peter the most extraordinary licence, not to mention undercover police assistance. This is the world of the monocle concealing a powerful magnifying lens, and the collapsible ruler hidden inside the walking-cane, as it is also the rather moving world of Great War veterans, Club servants with only one arm, and a vital clue in the form of the absence, on the victim's overcoat, of an Armistice Day poppy. The plotting is meticulous, though the identity of the murderer eminently guessable; every man and woman wears a hat and gloves; and solicitors refuse to entertain the notion of having their offices invaded by the telephone.

When I was eighteen, I went up to King's College, London, to read English, which at that time progressed in an entirely linear, chronological way from Anglo-Saxon to Dickens. Thereafter, various aspects of modern literature could be taken as Special Options and one of them was the Detective Story, taken seriously by academics even then, and much favoured. Dorothy L. Sayers featured on the syllabus, along with other women – Marjorie Allingham, Ngaio Marsh, Christie. I did not take the option myself but I read a good many of those detective stories as light relief from the rigours of *Beowulf*, Chaucer and Marlowe, Pope and Dryden.

They were almost always either the green Penguins, or the bright yellow detective stories published by Victor Gollancz in uniform, extremely ugly, jackets which never had pictures on them but were strictly lettering only. The Gollancz books I borrowed either from the old red-brick pile that was then the Kensington Public Library, or from somewhere far more illustrious, the august London Library in St James's Square.

The green Penguin detective stories were in a bookcase in the hostel where I lived for my three undergraduate years, opposite the Natural History Museum. It was run by a minor order of rather haughty and snobbish nuns, and one of them had brought her father's collection of Penguin Books into the house when he died. I was told it contained every Penguin detective story issued and I can well believe it. I read my way steadily through the lot, as did my room-mate, a music student from my native Yorkshire who became my instant and lasting best friend. Many of them were set in a London which then (1960) had barely changed since the time in which they were written. The docks were still the docks, and the Port of London one of the busiest commercial ports in the world; the river that ran past my college was packed with working boats and barges. Fleet Street was down the road and the printing presses still produced the papers from there – turn up a side alley and a door opening off the street looked down into a Dante's Inferno of noise and roaring machinery. There were bowler hats in the City and in all the lawyers' offices and barristers' chambers of Gray's Inn and Temple; boys with stubs of pencils behind their ears running about with early evening papers, shouting the headlines; coster-mongers in Covent Garden, and flowers in the flower market. Walk through King Street and someone would throw you a cheerful apple, further along, a carnation. In winter, roast-chestnut braziers glowed through the fog. The London Particular was in its dying days and it was not pleasant, though it has grown golden in the memory. It was dangerous, it tasted foul, it penetrated your lungs and turned a minor cold into bronchitis. But it is the pea-souper of *The Unpleasantness at the Bellona Club*, with old men tottering through it to the lantern which gleams its fuzzy welcome out of the whiteness, that, reading the book now, I can taste on my tongue.

Today's crime novel and police procedural is far more graphic than the detective story ever was and yet there is an exhumation in *The Bellona Club* which, with its subtle suggestions and hints of little things heard and seen as the men go about their grim work, is somehow, infinitely more unsettling than the full-on description by one of today's popular writers of a headless, hand-less, disembowelled murder victim.

I finished the Sayers novel while still sitting in the autumn sun and made a note to look for more. Wimsey has never been my favourite fictional detective. The silly-ass pose sits better on Bertie Wooster, whose chinless features never concealed a razor-sharp brain, and the Wimsey–Harriet Vane love story is embarrassing, but when I put *The Bellona Club* back in its box, I went in search of *The Nine Tailors* (probably Sayers' masterpiece) and *Murder Must Advertise.* They were not in the Small Dark Den. (I found them much later and in quite another corner of the house.)

Meanwhile, let us cross the den and open a small door which, like the one in the back of the wardrobe that led into Narnia, now gives out not into our hall, as it really should, but into the book stacks of the London Library.

# A Corner of St James's

IT IS ALWAYS the Michaelmas term. It is always early dark with lights shining out of a thousand London windows. It is always cold and the air always smells of smoke. It is always foggy. I am always nineteen or twenty. I am always wearing my King's College royal blue and scarlet scarf. (Was mine the last generation to sport them? It was the first thing we bought on arriving, and in the Strand and down Surrey Street they knew when term had begun by the sighting of the first scarf, like the first swallow. Many things may be better there now, and I am not a sentimentalist about my university days, but it was a sad one when things went into reverse, and, instead of being an object of pride, the wide, warm, striped college scarf became one of ridicule.)

The old Library in the Strand building at King's was an excellent place but during term time the waiting list for essential books on the reading schedule was very long. They had three copies each of E.M.W. Tillyard's *The Elizabethan World Picture* and *The Complete Essays of Hazlitt* but there were thirty of us needing them both and even if I had had any money to buy books, there were precious few second-hand copies available to be bought – or not until the end of the year, when they were no longer needed.

Then one day, waiting to check a book in or out, I caught sight of a notice about the London Library, 14 St James's Square, SW – of which I had never heard. Below a brief description of the Library, I read about a scholarship offered to full-time undergraduates. Get a scholarship and membership was free for the three years of one's degree course.

It was October and dark early. It was foggy. It was cold. I wore my royal blue and scarlet scarf. And I walked into that historic Library for the very first time to pick up an application form, knowing, as I did so – I had read up about the Library – that I was walking in the footsteps of George Eliot and T.S. Eliot, Charles Darwin and Charles Dickens, Kipling and Carlyle, Virginia Woolf and Vita Sackville-West, Henry James and M.R. James … and, oh, everyone, everyone, heroes all, a roll call of great writers.

My application had to be sponsored by two existing London Library Members and by my Head of Department at King's, Professor Geoffrey Bullough.

I took the form and headed to the Cromwell Road and the home of two writers who had become my friends and patrons, C.P. Snow and his wife, Pamela Hansford Johnson. They signed my application form, Charles Snow wrote an accompanying letter of recommendation, and, a very short time later, I was walking back to 14 St James's Square again for the first time as a London Library Student Member.

I have never been a country member of the Library. The joy of it was going there several times a week during term, collecting the books I needed to study, using the quiet corners in which to work – college libraries are not good for concentration, there is too much activity.

I think I learned as much from browsing in the book stacks of the London Library as I have done anywhere in my reading life. There is something extraordinarily liberating and exciting about being let loose in such a place, allowed to wander, pick out this and that, read a bit here, a page there, take out the book, then wander to another bay in search of something related to it. It is the self-education among books that few people, now, are privileged to have. Virginia Woolf describes the benefits of it in her *Diaries* and *Essays*, though in spite of being a member of the London Library later in life, her early book-education took place in her father's library in their house in Hyde Park Gate, one of the great private libraries of that, or any other, day.

But it was not only books I encountered in those somewhat perilous stacks and I daresay that it is the same now; for every eminent writer worth the name is a member, and a contemporary student might bump into Tom Stoppard or Antonia Fraser or David Hare and be star-struck.

One of the latter-day writers of the Golden Age style of detective story was Nicholas Blake – the pseudonym of the then Poet Laureate C. Day Lewis. It was easier for writers to go about unrecognised in those days, when television was in its infancy and the papers did not back up everything with a visual image, but Cecil Day Lewis could rarely have gone incognito because he had the most memorable of faces, lined and wrinkled like a map, as well as a rather large head. So when he stood aside for me to pass him in the narrow LL bookstacks I was hyper-conscious of who he was.

Not, though, as conscious as I was of the small man with thinning hair and a melancholy moustache who dropped a book on my foot in the Elizabethan Poetry section some weeks later. There was a small flurry of exclamations and apology and demur as I bent down, painful foot notwithstanding, picked up the book and handed it back to the elderly gentleman – and found myself looking into the watery eyes of E.M. Forster. How to explain the impact of that moment? How to stand and smile and say nothing, when through my head ran the opening lines of *Howards End*, 'One may as well begin with Helen's letters', alongside vivid images from the Marabar Caves of *A Passage to India*? How to take in that here, in a small space among old volumes and a moment when time stood still, was a man who had been an intimate friend of Virginia Woolf? He wore a tweed jacket. He wore, I think, spectacles that had slipped down his nose. He seemed slightly stooping and wholly unmemorable and I have remembered everything about him for nearly fifty years.

I went back to the hostel and took out *Where Angels Fear to Tread*, read some pages, read the author biography, and had that sense of unreality that comes only a few times in one's life. The wonder of the encounter has never faded. Nor, indeed, has the wonder of bumping into T.S. Eliot on the front doorstep of a house in Highgate, though, strangely, I cannot now remember *whose* house, but there was a literary party to which I had been invited by some kind patron of young writers. So there I stood, while Eliot rang the bell and gave me a rather owlish but kindly smile as we waited. Once the door was opened to us he was absorbed into the throng and I saw him no more – but I can certainly still hear the voice of someone saying, on seeing him, 'Oh good, here's Possum!'

# Saturday Mornings and Wednesday Afternoons

GIRLS READ MORE than boys, always have, always will. That's a known fact. But does the trend continue upwards with age? The answer is what the answer so often is – 'it all depends'. It all depends on the men and the women and the books and on who is asking the question and when. My guess is that more women read books than men. I can't prove this, of course, but I found two books on a top shelf, next to some full of untried recipes, which do provide a glimpse into the world of women and reading in which I grew up. I opened one of these, *The Feminine Middlebrow Novel, 1920s to 1950s*, and there they were, the authors whose novels my mother read. Lettice Cooper, E. Arnot Robinson, Jan Struther, Angela Thirkell, Pearl Buck, Enid Bagnold, Margaret Kennedy, Warwick Deeping, Mazo de la Roche, Winifred Holtby, Stella Gibbons, Frances Parkinson Keyes, Nevil Shute, John Galsworthy. Middlebrow and, for the most part, Middle England.

I was born and brought up in Scarborough, among the sort of women who, like my mother, went to Boots Circulating Library, which we did every Wednesday afternoon. Private libraries flourished then, alongside the public ones, even quite tiny ones run by a single lady from the backroom of her haberdashery or stationer's shop. Boots was the largest, a private library chain, and there, while my mother changed her copy of *The Chronicles of Jalna* for *The Constant Nymph*, I changed Noel Streatfield's *Ballet Shoes* for Pamela Brown's *Golden Pavements* – then, as now, small girls wanted to be ballerinas or actresses. When I had finished reading my book, which was always too soon, I used to try to read the ones my mother had borrowed but found them dull – domestic stories of women, love and families for the most part, for my mother was not one to stray into foreign parts or exotic adventures. So far as I remember, the books did not have dust jackets – perhaps they were stripped of them on arrival in the library, by the women at the desk, whose hair was coiled into earphones and who each wore a beige cardigan. The book covers were maroon, dark green, dark blue, with the Boots Circulating Library stamp inside. And they always smelled – they smelled of the women who borrowed them, of camphor and mothballs, boiled wool and cooking and cigarette smoke and some other unidentifiable but unmistakeable fusty, musty smell which was released like a faint gas when the cover was opened.

I have just read *Madame Claire* by Susan Ertz, a good novel which my mother, surely, must have read before me (though mine is a modern reprint). It is full of women who wear furs for every day. Madame Claire lives very contentedly in a hotel suite, looked after by her maid Dawson, and oversees the lives of her children and grandchildren in a benign, amused and rather detached way, as they fall in love, try to salvage something from the wreck of an unhappy marriage, plunge into unfortunate business ventures – and always come to Kensington to confide in her. It sounds a dull book but although its confines are limited, it has as much human interest as the novels of Barbara Pym, who worked on a similar miniature canvas to considerable effect.

The sum of these women's novels is almost always greater than their parts, as was discovered when Lord David Cecil presented Barbara Pym to the world all over again in a *Times Literary Supplement* article about unjustly neglected writers. The poet Philip Larkin championed her in the same place and, as a result, she had a late flowering into bestsellerdom in the 1970s. They were precisely the kind of books my mother would have borrowed and better than many that she did. Pym's world of stuttering curates, wistful spinsters and awkward bachelors, of North Oxford and small country parishes, is superficially bland and narrow. What makes it of greater importance is her trenchant eye, her detached and sometimes mordant vision of these well-meaning, fumbling people at odds with so much of life. She is good on petty jealousy, hidden sorrow, unvoiced love, genteel regret, middle-class poverty. And on curates. I have her novels on the paperback shelves in the sitting room, for once set neatly together under P, though, inexplicably, in the middle of a row of modern European drama by Ionesco, Genet and Brecht.

'Would I like Barbara Pym? Where should I start?' Anywhere, really. Odd that. It is not always the case. You should never begin reading George Eliot with *Middlemarch*, nor Trollope with *The Way we Live Now*, and one of the lesser Muriel Sparks might put you off

for good. But Barbara Pym is Barbara Pym. Try *Quartet in Autumn*.
On the other hand, start with *Jane and Prudence*. You will know
within, say, thirty pages, whether she is your cup of tea or not, and
if not, then that is probably that. I am glad I did not read *The Mill
on the Floss* first or I would never have tried another George Eliot,
and *Travels with my Aunt* is not a typical novel by Graham Greene,
so it does not much matter if you do not care for it. But any Barbara
Pym will give you the idea. If you like her, just read on.

I do not know if more people read now than they did in the
1940s and 1950s, but I am certain they go to the library less often.
The old private ones no longer exist of course, and public libraries
have changed, in many cases for the worse. There are fewer new
books to borrow, old ones have been de-commissioned (that is,
thrown out), computers have arrived, as have reading glasses for
sale and DVDs for rent. There are children's sections in libraries
and they are often the best, most popular part, but are there separate buildings called 'The Children's Library' any longer? There
was one in Scarborough, attached, but separate from, the main
lending and reference libraries and when we arrived there every
Saturday morning, my mother walked in at one side while I walked
down to the other. If the private library had Boots' stamps and
stickers, the public children's library sometimes had labels on a
book declaring that it had been fumigated. Infectious and conta-
gious diseases were still rife then. Chickenpox. Measles. Scarlet
fever. Tuberculosis. Mumps. Whooping cough. Children died of
them. Books that went into infected houses might be returned
thick with germs, so it was necessary to report certain illnesses
when books were returned, so that they could be put into special
fumigation chambers to be rendered clean and safe again.

It was in the Scarborough Children's Public Library that I discovered not only the Bobbsey twins and *Anne of Green Gables*, the stories of Malcolm Saville, *Huckleberry Finn* and Lamb's *Tales from Shakespeare*. Most wonderful of all, I discovered Enid Blyton.

Enid Blyton's books did for my generation, and several generations since, what J.K. Rowling's have done recently – broke that invisible barrier between children who are natural-born readers and children who are not. Unless they have been adversely influenced by an adult, no child has ever felt ashamed of being seen with a Harry Potter, though they might never admit to reading any other book. Adults may say what they like – parents, teachers and other know-alls. Enid Blyton excited us, took us into worlds of mystery, magic, adventure and fun. Yes, her prose is bland, yes, the vocabulary is not particularly stretching. But Blyton had the secret, the knack. I missed out on the Noddy books though not on the *Magic Faraway Tree*, but my real Blytons were the stories of the Famous Five, the Secret Seven, the Mystery of … series and the boarding school world of Malory Towers. I lived with those boys and girls, who were around my own age but lived far more interesting lives, with nicer houses, more fun parents, greater freedom to gallop about the countryside on horses, take out boats and bikes, and go hiking and mountain climbing. There were villains, there was danger, they got into scrapes, yet their world was essentially serene and safe and for the duration of the story I, like many thousands of other readers between the ages of seven and twelve or so, was wholly absorbed in it. These were my friends and companions, I was one of the Five and the Seven, I went to the Mountain of Adventure and Spooky Cottage, I was in the Fifth at Malory Towers. We all were. Blyton taught me what books could do, where the imagination could take me, how I could be transported to other places, know the sort of people I might never know in reality and learn about how the world of friendship and sibling relationships worked, too – a vital lesson for an only child. I still do not understand why Blyton has been frowned upon by adults for so many years. What is there to disapprove of, what is harmful? Limited, yes, but what book does not have its limits? My mother preached against Blyton while reading a light-romantic author called Naomi Jacob, for heaven's sake.

Most of my Blytons were library books so I do not have any on my shelves now – except one, the book I received for Christmas when I was five and a half. It has a bright-green cloth binding with the lettering, *Enid Blyton's Treasury*, in gold, and the spine is weak from being opened too many times. There are just two books which have the power to catapult me back sixty years into childhood – *Alice in Wonderland*, and this. When I open it I am transported, by the titles and the stories and the line illustrations, in the most extraordinary way – the way of the Proustian madeleine. *The Mystery of Melling Cottage, A Night on Thunder Rock*, and, perhaps most evocative of all, *The Wild West Kids*, in which some children join a circus for a day. Circuses were circuses then, with real lions and tigers and the roar and smell of danger. Bertram Mills Circus visited Scarborough every year, arriving with a parade through the town, just like the one in my book. Real life and fiction merged. For two pins I would have run away to join the circus. I still might.

That one remaining Blyton book of the dozens I read happens to sit next to *Harry Potter and the Goblet of Fire*. But whereas adults read Harry P, I doubt if many ever read Blyton, except aloud in the form of a bedtime story. Rowling's world of magic seems to cross every age barrier. I once came home late, when the rest of the household were in bed, and, even though they were fully adult, I still went in to check that the two daughters had not died a cot death. That night I found them, aged twenty-three and fifteen, and a husband, aged a lot older, each tucked up reading a different Harry Potter. Of how many authors, living or dead, might one say that?

# Next to the Pop-Up Books

The handsome creature comes to rest,
Accepts the Orchid's proffered best,
He sips the nectar rare. Now gently turn the page between,
The striking couple will be seen. Then close the book with care.

IT IS NOT EASY to convey, in a world stuffed full of new books in high streets papered with bookshops, how rare and exotic a thing a brand-new book was to a child born during the war, and learning to read and to love books and stories in the 1940s and early 1950s. Books came printed on poor, thin, almost transparent paper, and bore a horrid official stamp announcing that they conformed to Government War Standards, and they were not easy to come by.

But Christmas always brought at least a couple – the longed-for *Rupert Bear Annual* and another, about two characters called Japhet and Happy. Rupert, with his friends Pong-Ping and Tiger Lily, and his yellow- and black-checked scarf, is still going strong. I used to memorise page after page of the story-rhymes, which were so easy to get by heart. But Japhet and Happy, created by the *News Chronicle* cartoonist Frank Horrabin, and part of a series about the Noah Family, have disappeared. Annuals were an essential part of childhood; indeed, *The Beano Annual* continues to appear in my Christmas stocking every year.

But in 1948, when I was six, I was given a book that was quite different to anything I had ever seen in my young life, a book so magical I could hardly breathe when I opened it; it was a book that began a collection to which I still add, and which I often spend five minutes (or twenty-five minutes) opening and enjoying.

My first pop-up book was the latest of a series which had begun in 1929, by another man working in newspapers – S. Louis Giraud, who came from the production department of the *Daily Express* to invent the *Bookano* series – the first truly 'automatic' books. The name was a take on the famous Meccano construction sets consisting of little bits of metal with holes in them, to be joined by screws and washers, and supposedly capable of being made into everything, including St Paul's Cathedral, from a skyscraper to an aircraft carrier. Its literary counterpart, *Bookano*, was an anthology of fictional stories and tales from history with some coloured pictures, but the real joy of the series was, and is, the pop-ups. They were not called pop-ups then, they were described by a sentence which scans so perfectly you cannot help chanting it every time you say the word 'Bookano … with Pictures that Spring up in Model Form'.

I still have three of my old *Bookanos*. They are well-read, well-loved, well-handled, though the pictures that spring up in model form are all intact. I must have been very careful with them. Modern paper-engineering has come many a mile since these simple creations, but, to my eyes, the *Bookano* Westminster Abbey and Tower Bridge and a working windmill rising up magnificently from between the ordinary printed pages still take the breath away with surprise. That is what a pop-up book should do – take the breath away for a single, amazing moment which can be repeated again and again.

It was *Bookano* that taught me to love the pop-up book and my year of reading from home was enlivened by the time I spent going through my collection. Some are educational, some are the stuff of fantasy, some are babyish, and others are for grown-ups (there is, though I do not own it, a pop-up *Kama Sutra*).

I had started my journey in Indian summer weather but two days later we had a monsoon, with dark grey clouds like lead balloons weighing down the sky, so I spread some of my favourite pop-up books on the kitchen table, to play with them there.

Robert Sabuda is the modern master of the pop-up. His paper engineering is intricate, detailed and incredibly beautiful and, as his home country, the USA, has so many marvels which lend themselves so well to the form, I put his amazing *America the Beautiful* at the top of the pile. Open it. Here are the Great Plains, represented by a pop-up corn mill and waves of paper grain which pop up in rows. Here is the most wondrous Mississippi river boat. All of these pop-ups are cut from stark-white paper card and the finest of all is New York: skyscrapers, Statue of Liberty, and here, shrouded in a small envelope to one corner, the Twin Towers.

The idea of turning *Moby-Dick* into a three-dimensional graphic novel (by paper-engineer Sam Ita) was a clever one, and best of all I love the ship's deck from which pops up a pulpit, a preacher, a rows of sailors each holding a pop-up Bible; and, when the whole boat pops up, complete with sails all carefully held by thin cotton threads, the effect is breathtaking.

Our own master paper-engineer and storyteller combined is Jan Pienkowski. I sat happily opening and closing his *Fungus the Bogeyman Plop-up Book*, *Robot* and *Haunted House* while the rain streamed down the windows. What more could book-life hold?

# Great Expectations
# Behind the Sofa

IT WAS ONE of the reasons that I married my husband (along with discovering that we each had photographs of ourselves aged three riding a donkey on Scarborough sands – possibly the same donkey, twelve years apart). He told me quite early on, possibly even the first time we met, that he had read *Pickwick Papers* when he was eleven, sitting on the floor behind the sofa of his family house.

With me it was *Great Expectations,* and the sofa – beige moquette with lace antimacassars, as sofas were – belonged to my great-aunt, whose bungalow in a leafy avenue of Southport we often visited. Southport and scenes from Dickens are intertwined forever in my mind. I have read Dickens over and over ever since, but have not re-visited Southport since the 1950s. Beryl Bainbridge, who knew it in the same period, wrote that it had lost its character, to become 'just like anywhere else'. My great-aunt was the reader and my great-uncle, who had been blind from his teens, listened to talking books on a huge, horned gramophone. These arrived with the postman, free to borrow, free to return, then as now, but then were in dozens, like great, round black plates, and they were delivered in huge boxes tied with leather straps and buckles. I can still hear Churchill's voice booming out of the microphone, as he read his memoirs and speeches aloud to my uncle.

The actual books in the house were few, and probably the glass-fronted case and its contents were duplicated in front parlours across the land – the Bible, a five-volume encyclopaedia, the *Oxford English Dictionary*, Palgrave's *Golden Treasury*, *Roget's Thesaurus*, a ready reckoner, and the complete works of William Shakespeare, Charles Dickens and Sir Walter Scott.

I have just been down to the sitting room to look at that same set of Dickens, which my great-aunt finally gave to me when I was twelve because, she said, I obviously got more out of it than she ever would. I have three other complete sets, and now I read the Oxford, in hardback, because it has the original Boz and Phiz illustrations but rather better print. My great-aunt's set is bound in speckled brown, the titles are in gold, and the pages have yellowed with age. The paper is of poor quality so that the print is unclear, and it is very small. I do not wear glasses for reading but the type is too small for me all the same. But sometimes I like to open *Bleak House* or *The Old Curiosity Shop* and leaf through a few pages because they still smell of my great-aunt's house and the warm den behind the sofa.

I could spend my year of reading from home with Dickens alone – well, almost. In the silly game of which authors to throw overboard from the lifeboat and which one – just one – to save, I would always save Dickens. He is mighty. His flaws are huge but magnificent – and all of a piece with the whole. A perfect, flawless Dickens would somehow be a shrunken, impoverished one. Yes, he is sentimental, yes, he has purple passages, yes, his plots sometimes have dropped stitches, yes, some of his characters are quite tiresome. But his literary imagination was the greatest ever, his world of teeming life is as real as has ever been invented, his conscience, his passion for the underdog, the poor, the cheated, the humiliated are god-like. He created an array of varied, vibrant, living, breathing men and women and children that is breathtaking in its scope. His scenes are painted like those of an Old Master, in vivid colour and richness on huge canvases. His prose is spacious, symphonic, infinitely flexible. He can portray evil and create a menacing atmosphere of malevolence better than any other writer – read *Little Dorrit*, read *Our Mutual Friend*, read *Bleak House* if you don't believe me. He is macabre, grotesque, moralistic, thunderous, funny, ridiculous, heartfelt. Nobody has ever written as he wrote about London, nobody has described the Essex Marshes so well, nobody has opened a book to such effect as he does in *Bleak House*. There is no area of life he does not illuminate, no concern or cause he does not make his own, no sentences, no descriptions, no exchanges, no sadnesses or tragedies or betrayals …

There are one or two of his novels that I never want to read again, A *Tale of Two Cities* being the first. I don't think he felt comfortable writing historical fiction, and it shows. Though I am glad to have read it, I am happy to leave *David Copperfield* on the shelf, in spite of Mr Micawber, and my husband is welcome to laugh at Pickwick because I never could …

But look at what is left. One of my Complete Dickens sets has introductions by Peter Ackroyd which are always worth re-reading, and among the academic literary criticism I sometimes return to, John Carey's brilliant study of Dickens's imagination, *The Violent Effigy*, has a place at High Table. Ah, John Carey. The man never writes a dull word and I cherish the article on the joys of vegetable gardening which he wrote years ago for *The Times* as much as his books on Donne and the wonderfully thought-provoking, and provocative, *What Use are the Arts?* When a first-rate mind and a razor-sharp command of the language come together, the result is formidable. If laughter is the best medicine, a bracing mental walk with a writer like John Carey is a top tonic.

I started my re-read through Dickens with a short novel, *Great Expectations*. Anyone would do well to begin there and then go on to the mighty and moving, though untypical *A Christmas Carol* – best read, of course, on 24 December. After that, it is time I went back to *Little Dorrit*. Is it the best? I sometimes think so. Then again, I change my mind. *Bleak House* is the greatest of all the novels. But *Our Mutual Friend* has, I think, absolutely no flaws, and there is something about its descriptions of London's river at its blackest, most secret, most terrifying, and the low life that lurked about its quays and alleys and pot-houses, that takes me back to those Michaelmas terms, and the chill mist drifting off the Thames.

> Fog everywhere. Fog up the river, where it flows among green aits and meadows; fog down the river, where it rolls defiled among the tiers of shipping, and the waterside pollutions of a great (and dirty) city. Fog on the Essex marshes, fog on the Kentish heights ...

Outside my window, the trees are bare. It is early dark but a silver paring of moon is bright in the sky, with a thousand frosty stars. The air smells of cold. A fox barks from the field.

Dickens for winter.

Throw another log on the fire.

# This is the Weather the Cuckoo Likes

LOOKING FOR a Latin dictionary, I came upon a faded and battered small anthology called *A Child's Garland*, which was collected together for a small girl called Polly Carton who was sent to Canada at the age of eight to escape the horrors of wartime London. It contains a selection of adult verse and prose but, as the editor says, 'nothing in which a child may not delight'. Well, a child of those times at least. I was given my copy when I too was eight. I do not now remember how I reacted to the bits from Spenser or Sir Henry Newbolt but I do have a lot of the poetry in it by heart, as I have a good many chunks from Palgrave's *Golden Treasury*. And lest it should be thought what a good little girl I was, I hasten to explain that, on the contrary, so much of the poetry I still remember was learned by heart because I was extremely naughty. If you were as badly behaved as I was at my convent school, you were given a detention. There was a period when I can barely ever have arrived home at the right time: I was in almost permanent detention. Two punishments were meted out during these solitary periods in the classroom when the rest of the school had fallen quiet. One was to hem sheets by hand, as a result of which I acquired such a loathing of needle and thread that I have refused to ply them at any time in the course of my adult life. But the other, and more frequently meted out, punishment was to learn a poem and recite it word perfect at the end of the detention period. The nun on detention duty chose the poems and many of them are right here, in *A Child's Garland* and Palgrave. I learned poetry by the yard. Tennyson, Keats, Browning, Kipling, Shelley, de la Mare, Wordsworth … 'Season of mist and mellow fruitfulness … The splendour falls on castle walls … Tiger, Tiger burning bright … From the troubles of the world, I turn to ducks … Do you remember an Inn, Miranda, do you remember an Inn … John Gilpin was a citizen/Of credit and renown …'

In times of stress, waiting in a long traffic jam or to go under the dental drill, I lower my blood pressure by reciting the whole of 'The Lady of Shalott'.

'On either side the river lie,
Long fields of barley and of rye.'

Oh, don't start me.

I get great pleasure from knowing so much poetry – though much of it should rather be called, simply, verse, because the rhymes and rhythms are so soothing and satisfying. And it is a terrific help when doing crosswords and answering quizzes at Christmas. The ability to learn by heart, like the solving of really complex maths, is a young gift and it burns out pretty early, though I got a great deal of John Donne and W.H. Auden by heart when I was studying them for A level – no textbooks in the exam room in those days, so if you wanted to quote you had to learn it.

It was my ability to recite quite a lot of poetry that helped me both into and smartly out of a conversation with Edith Sitwell – possibly the most awkward conversation I have ever had in my life.

The Sitwells, Osbert, Edith and Sacheverell, children of Sir George and all of them writers, once lived in Scarborough, too, in a house called Wood End, where there used to be a room kept as they had known it, containing copies of their books and manuscripts and the great portrait by Sargent of the three of them as children. We went to the Sitwell House, and to the Art Gallery next door, on many a Sunday afternoon, with tea afterwards in the Gallery, and after wandering round the strange museum part of Wood End, looking at old bits of flint and Roman coins, I was always waiting to dodge away into the Sitwell room to look at their picture. They fascinated me even then, with their extraordinary, arrestingly beautiful-ugly, bony aquiline faces and Edwardian clothes. My favourite was Sacheverell – or Sachie – because of his name. I got to know him well thirty years later, when I went to interview him for a BBC programme about Scarborough and we sat swapping stories of the place – remembering the wind roaring round the chimney pots, having croup and bronchitis, smelling camphorated oil, walking along the beach with eyes down in case there was a golden coin among the pebbles. We had the same memories, so many years apart. The house in which I was born was a pebble's throw from the one in which they had lived. Sachie could never get over it. 'We looked at the same roof slates and walked on the same paving slabs,' he once said. Sachie loved Scarborough and would have talked about it and his childhood there for ever, as I would have listened. The others did not love it, as I was to find out when I walked into the drawing room of Charles and Pamela Snow's flat one evening and saw Edith Sitwell sitting bolt upright in a chair at the far end. Imagine it. Queen Elizabeth the First or the Queen of Sheba, definitely someone very royal, silk turban, amazingly coloured garments draped about her person. Rings, huge rings, vast gold chains and bracelets everywhere. And that face. The same face I knew so well from the Sargent portrait but grown up and grown old. Her eyes were the most extraordinary eyes I have ever seen, huge, heavily lidded, mesmerising, half-closed like the eyes of an apparently sleeping but terribly watchful crocodile.

And there was I, eighteen, a university student. But I had just published my first novel, which might have made me of very slightly more interest to Edith. Only it did not.

The eyelids half closed. The long bony fingers tapped on the arm of the chair. The rings flashed in the light of the lamp. My throat went very dry.

I blurted out that I was born and grew up in Scarborough, that I knew their house so well, so well. I wished I could have explained to her the fascination it had had for me, the way I had been haunted by them, by their portrait. Their names.

'I hated Scarborough,' she said.

'Wood End …'

'I loathed that house.'

There was absolutely nothing whatsoever that I could say.

'Do you read poetry?' she asked.

'Oh yes.'

'Do you get it by heart?'

I did not explain how I had done so, but I said that yes, I knew a lot of poetry by heart. Was she expecting me to say that I knew poetry of hers? I did, actually, I knew 'Still Falls the Rain', but I was too nervous to say so. Probably I should have done but she might have told me she hated it now, loathed the poem.

I do not know if Edith Sitwell ever laughed – possibly not. Somehow, that face was always haughty, disdainful, solemn, watchful of expression, though the eyes might have flickered and glinted with amusement. So I was spared the humiliation of any sort of laughter when I replied to her next question.

'What do you know by heart?'

I was not prepared. I was terrified. Thrown. Totally unsure of what or how to answer, though a second's pause for calm thought would have allowed me to collect myself and say 'Spenser. Chaucer. Shakespeare.' But the effect of Edith Sitwell a foot away from me, Queen Elizabeth the First re-incarnated, did not allow me to pause calmly for thought. I did not plan what I would say in reply. One never does at such moments. I opened my mouth and out came

'This is the weather the cuckoo likes,
And so do I.
When showers betumble the chestnut spikes
And nestlings fly.
And the little brown nightingale builds his nest
And ...'

The expression on her face is one I shall remember until my dying day. I fled.

Years later, I told Sachie the story, sitting in the eminently comfortable drawing room in Northamptonshire. He had the same face as Edith, same nose, same eyes, though his were not so hooded and they laughed. He laughed now, hooting down his nose and inhaling his cigarette at the same time, tossing his head back. The laugh said everything but it was not unkind, not scornful, not dismissive. It was a laugh which told me that he summed up the whole scene in one, his sister's expression, my horror and embarrassment, the awful Hardy verses somehow coming out of their own accord and too late to get them back. He did not need to say a single word. The laugh was enough.

I do not read much poetry now, and rarely anything new. I know I should. Should. Ought. But I don't and that's that. Perhaps I don't need to. I can recite the whole of 'The Lady of Shalott' after all, and W.H. Auden's:

'As I walked out one evening,
Walking down Bristol Street,
The crowds upon the pavement
Were fields of harvest wheat.'

And

'The curfew tolls the knell of parting day.'

And

'Slowly, silently now, the moon
Walks the night in her silver shoon.'

Or perhaps

> 'Whenever the moon and stars are set
> Whenever the wind is high,
> All night long in the dark and wet
> A man goes riding by …'

And then again, there is

> 'If you wake at midnight,
> And hear a horse's feet,
> Don't go drawing back the blind
> Or looking in the street.'

It's a comfort to know that when I am old and grey and full of tears, I will still be able to say:

> 'This is the weather the cuckoo likes.'

By heart.

But not all the poetry I know was learned when I was a child. I did not encounter Charles Causley's work until I was fully adult but he is a poet whose verses stick like burrs to the inside of the mind. I don't remember making any attempt to learn them, I just absorbed them by osmosis.

> 'I had a silver penny and an apricot tree
> And I said to the sailor on the white quay …'

It sounds like a poem for children. So do others.

Ah, people said, Charles Causley, 'the children's poet'. The tone was always patronising. And indeed, he wrote poetry for children, some of the best in English. So, of course, did Ted Hughes, about whom no one ever dared speak patronisingly. But there is nothing sweet or charming or, well, patronising, about the poems either of them wrote for the young. You will have to think for only a few seconds, surely, before remembering the opening lines of Causley's best-known, most anthologised poem about, and for, someone young:

> Timothy Winters comes to school,
> With eyes as wide as a football pool,
> Ears like bombs and teeth like splinters,
> A blitz of a boy is Timothy Winters.

Causley could no more write down to children than he could sentimentalise them. He wasn't a primary schoolteacher for thirty-odd years for nothing. 'Children,' he said, clear-eyed as ever, 'you walk among them at your peril.'

But he wished he had had his own. He wrote a letter to me a few years ago, one of many wonderful, rich, funny and revealing letters, in which he talked about Hughes, his greatest friend, about how he had loved him, how he missed him.

'I used to see them often, when he was with Sylvia. Lovely girl. And Frieda and Nicholas. I used to look at them in their cots and think, "and all I've got to show for it are a few old poems".'

Occasionally, because he was a lifelong bachelor, people thought he was homosexual. It troubled him. When A.L. Rowse told

Causley, 'You're one of us,' he said to me, 'I hope he only meant a Cornishman.' He would have married, he said, if …

The pause was a silent reference to his mother; he was pretty well chained by her during her lifetime, though he made dashes for the open world, to Canada and Australia and Asia, a term here, a term there, as visiting writer and poet in residence.

I first saw him in 1971 at the famous Book Bang in Bedford Square when he was receiving a poetry prize, and I said to a mutual friend, the poet William Plomer, that he looked melancholy.

'He has reason,' Plomer said, 'he has a Mother.'

He was not melancholy, really, or rather, not in company, not in letters, not in our phone calls, which grew longer and more frequent as he became housebound after a series of strokes, and then went into a home in his native Launceston. He loved talking about books, poetry, children, life, the literary world he was, and yet was not, a part of. He always made me laugh. His turn of phrase was unique, and throwaway lines, spoken in his slight Cornish burr, were either achingly funny or achingly memorable. He once spoke of a line of poetry that Hughes had written as so good 'it makes your hair catch fire'.

He made use of the legends and folklore of Cornwall all his writing life, in his children's poems and stories, and, most of all, in the ballads, which were for every age.

Very occasionally, the ballad form leads him into a kind of archness at odds with the rest of his work:

Mary stood in the kitchen
Baking a loaf of bread.
An angel flew in through the window
'We've a job for you,' he said.

Rarely does the Christianity that is the warp and woof of his verse fail to bring out the dark side in his poetry. The Christ-story was a bitter one for him, the person of Christ a suffering, betrayed human being, assayed by all the forces of evil. Even when the rhyme dances, the words are steeped in gall.

Watch where he comes walking
Out of the Christmas flame,
Dancing, double-talking:

Herod is his name.

War infuses his poetry. It was war that first took him far abroad from Cornwall as a young man and his finest verse was forged in the experience of the navy in wartime.

As he grew increasingly frail and nervous of leaving home, Causley began to receive some of the serious public recognition that should have been his years before – though his fellow poets always knew his worth. In 2000, three years before he died, he won the Heywood Hill Literary Prize for a Lifetime's Contribution to Literature, worth £15,000, and asked me if I would receive it on his behalf, and make the speech he had written.

I also read one of his great poems, 'Convoy', about a dead sailor:

Draw the blanket of ocean,
Over his frozen face.
He lies, his eyes quarried by glittering fish,
Staring through the green freezing sea-glass
At the Northern Lights.

He is now a child in the land of Christmas:
Watching, amazed, the white tumbling bears
And the diving seal.
The iron wind clangs round the ice-caps,
The five-point Dog-star
Burns over the silent sea,

And the three ships
Come sailing in.

When I told him about it he said, 'Oh that was terrible, Susan, I knew him all my life and then I came home and he didn't and I had to pass his mother every day in Launceston High Street. I always wished I'd turn to stone.'

He was never poor, never rich, but winning the Heywood Hill Prize meant more than honour to him. I asked if he would sign a book for a friend and mentioned that I was enclosing stamps for its return. 'No, no, please do not,' he said, 'money means nothing to me, now that I've won this prize. I can scatter it like bird seed.'

Remembering him, I remember the jokes. One always does. I also have one hilarious visual memory of him. We had taken part in a radio programme together one January, at the University of Exeter, to which he had been driven from Cornwall by a young German friend. We were all going out to supper afterwards and euphoric at having finished the work part of the evening, we came out of the main entrance into a world of snow. It was beautiful, but as he was marvelling at it, Causley leaped forward and descended to his waist into a drift. As we looked on in amazement, and horror, he said ruefully, his Cornish accent somehow strengthened by the drama of the moment, 'I don't know that we shall make dinner in public … I really am awfully wet.'

He was a man who made the most of things. Was he happy in old age? Probably not. He would have loved a wife, children, grand-children, and after his strokes, he relied on the help of his kind Launceston neighbours. He gave up walking to the corner shop on his Zimmer frame to buy Captain Birds Eye's frozen 'Ocean Pie' after he fell heavily. Soon, he knew he had to go into the home. His only worry was his cat. In the home, they were kind to him, hon-oured him even, and he told hilarious stories about the events of the day there. On one occasion, a man had visited from a local zoo, bringing pets with him. 'I never thought I'd end up with a blessed monkey in my arms,' he said ruefully.

I think he knew the value of his own work. But he was never vain, never anything but young in heart and spirit.

Shortly after receiving the Heywood Hill Prize, he was made a Companion of Literature by the Royal Society of Literature, a rare honour, and asked me, again, to accept on his behalf. 'What would you like me to say?' I asked.

The reply might well have been: 'What an honour.' Or perhaps, 'What a surprise …' But one of our greatest living poets, aged eighty-three, asked me to say, 'My goodness, what an encouragement.'

# The Well-Travelled Bookcase

MY FEW BOOKS of travel writing have gravitated towards one another over the years and stuck together out of solidarity, for there are not very many – I am not a traveller, nor even much of an armchair one, and it is some time since I read any of them, so now that it is deep midwinter, I am taking them down and dusting them off to see if I can be transported to warmer places, brighter days.

If I have to pick out just one travel writer, I guess I will not be alone in picking out the doyen of them all, Patrick Leigh Fermor.

The book of his I have re-read most often is hardly a travel book at all – or if it is, the travel is inwards, a spiritual journey. Some books are balm to the soul and solace to the weary mind, a cooling stream at the end of long, tiring days and *A Time to Keep Silence* is assuredly one of them. In the 1950s, PLF went from Paris to stay in two monasteries, St Wandrille and La Grande Trappe, in order to rest, recuperate from some crisis – he does not elaborate – and write a book. He was not a believer but he gained immeasurably in spirit, as well as in mind and body, from the accepting atmosphere, the silence, the calm routine and quiet presence of wholly – and holy – dedicated men. He saw the point of their way of life, though he could never share it, and so his book can give sustenance to any readers, believers or not, who can immerse themselves in its beautiful and reflective prose and allow themselves to rest there. It is a book that has never failed me, a companion over many years, in troubled times as well as good ones.

Moreover, this is a world which still exists. Visitors would still find life in a Trappist or a Benedictine monastery relatively unchanged. But the world through which PLF journeyed as a young man of eighteen, walking from the Hook of Holland to Constantinople, has changed almost entirely. He would not recognise much of it now which is what makes his classic accounts so precious. A *Time of Gifts* and *Between the Woods and the Water* are unsurpassed as travel books; page after page transport the reader to worlds so strange that they, and the people who inhabit them, might come from fairy tales. The place names are magical – Transylvania, the Carpathians, Constantinople – and this world seems far removed from the one which became the Eastern Europe of the post-war communist regimes and which is now divided, re-named and, in the aftermath of other wars, rapidly becoming part of a homogenised Euroland. But the glories of the blue mountains, fast-flowing rivers and the deep, dark forests lying across the hills like animal pelts which Leigh Fermor describes will not have changed, and besides, within his pages, as within those of all great travel writing, the world remains as it was then, and also timeless.

There is something about travellers and travel writers, some faraway look, some set of the eyes, some restlessness in their long

legs which are so accustomed to walking. You could tell that Bruce
Chatwin was a traveller and a nomad the moment you set eyes on
him, which I first did when he loped into a BBC Studio in 1986, to
record an interview for the Radio 4 programme *Bookshelf* which I
was then presenting.

Everyone has said it. He was astoundingly good looking, with
blonde hair and bluer than blue eyes and he had erudition coming
out of his ears, and the arrogant manner of a man who has been
adored all his life.

The book he was promoting was called *The Songlines*, and was
about Australian aborigines, in whom I had then, as now, little
interest. But when Bruce started to talk you were spellbound – he
could have been lecturing on the manufacture of brown paper bags
and you would still have been spellbound. If I did not take to that
particular book – which was criticised as well as praised for its
thesis about the Song Lines of the outback – it sent me to other
Chatwin titles and I fell in love with his writing, both travel – *In
Patagonia* – and fiction. He was a remarkable novelist. No book of
his is remotely like another and every one convinces the reader that
here is someone who knows as much about this story, these places,
these people, as it is possible to know – poor farmers of the Brecon
Beacons in *On the Black Hill*, a nineteenth-century African mogul
in *The Viceroy of Ouida*, a Czechoslovakian porcelain collector
called *Utz* … Chatwin was a maverick and a genius.

After the recording we chatted a bit and he mentioned in passing
that his parents lived in Stratford-upon-Avon – which turned out
to be half a dozen doors from where we had a small house. His
parents were the charming couple I often used to stop and talk to,
when I was going up the street with my daughter in her pushchair.

They were thrilled to know that I had met Bruce, listened to our radio interview, and were clearly immensely proud of him.

He walked out of the studio that day, tiny rucksack on his back, en route for the South of France – and from there, who knew? I used to hear news of him when I bumped into his parents – he was always somewhere exotic, somewhere of which I had barely heard.

The next time I saw Bruce himself I barely recognised him. I had met his father, who had said that Bruce was 'rather ill', but nothing more, and I had forgotten about it. At that time, around 1988, I was attending the Churchill Hospital, Oxford, every month, having de-sensitising treatment for my life-threatening wasp allergy in the dramatically named Venom Clinic. On the ward to which the clinic was attached, I was to learn later, Bruce had been looked after during the critical days of his diagnosis with AIDS, which was just beginning to wreak its havoc. It was, then, invariably fatal and it carried a great stigma. Nobody knew he had it – he put out a variety of weird and wonderful stories about the rare illness from which he was suffering, including one about having been poisoned after eating a one thousand-year-old egg in some obscure part of the Far East.

Well, why not? It was a good story, an utterly Chatwin story, romantic, rare, glamorous.

But the day I saw Bruce being wheeled down the corridor, I had no notion of any of that. It was simply quite clear to me that here was a man dying. The blue eyes burned out of hollow sockets, there was only a thin paint of flesh on his bones, his frame was bent over in the chair. He seemed very small. But when he saw me, his voice rang out as piercingly as ever, drawing attention to itself so that he was instantly the focus of everything. I don't remember what we said but it was a brief exchange. He told me that he and his wife had been all over the place, shopping, buying up 'dozens of beautiful, beautiful things'. It sounded slightly manic.

He waved a lordly hand and was gone. I knew that I would not see him again. But I had the books. They are here. I pick up *In Patagonia*. The cover has a quote from Paul Theroux: 'He has fulfilled the desire of all real travellers, of having found a place that is far and seldom visited, like the Land where the Jumblies live.'

Yes, that is exactly right, for Bruce would never have found anywhere that was ordinary or of our world.

The best travel writers make everywhere longed for, of course, a magic kingdom, for every one of them somehow invents their own places, so that when others go there, they are never quite as expected.

Colin Thubron has been everywhere – into the Lost Heart of Asia, by car, alone, from St Petersburg and the Baltic States south to Georgia and Armenia, by foot, bicycle and train from Beijing to Tibet (after having learned Mandarin), to the romantic ports and villages of Lebanon, into Siberia. Like Bruce Chatwin he has written novels, too. Like Leigh Fermor's, his travels are partly travels into depths of himself. Like both of them, he writes like an angel, and, the first time I saw him, I thought he was one, the most beautiful young man I had ever set eyes on.

I was eighteen. I had wanted to be a writer for as long as I could remember, and having filled the inevitable exercise books with bad short stories and worse poems, had written a novel. Looking back, I see that it was not a very good novel but it did have one merit – it was not in the least autobiographical, which many first novels are. Perhaps that was why it found a publisher. Which is why I was about to walk into the hallowed portals of Hutchinson, in London, to meet one of the great names of twentieth-century British publishing, Sir Robert Lusty, and the woman who was to be my editor, Dorothy Tomlinson. Her father, the novelist H.M. Tomlinson, had been a close friend of Thomas Hardy, which to me was like saying he sat at the right hand of God. Dorothy remembered him, though not well as he had died when she was a girl. But that she had met him and remembered him was enough for me.

Publishers' offices have not changed very much since 1960. There was a reception area, with some of the firm's books on display, and a girl behind a desk, with a typewriter and a telephone.

She said, 'Miss Tomlinson's assistant will come and fetch you.'

And a few moments later, Colin Thubron did.

I told Dorothy Tomlinson I thought her assistant the handsomest man I had ever seen and she agreed but she also doubted if he would be with her as a junior for long. He wanted to travel, she said, and write.

He did.

Colin has barely changed in fifty years. He has the same mane of hair, the same bony frame, the same long, striding traveller's legs, the same good looks, the same charm. He is still travelling, still writing.

How delightful. And somehow, very reassuring.

# Laughter in the Next Room

... AS OSBERT SITWELL called one of his volumes of autobiography. There they sit. I am not sure quite why, but thousands of households in the immediate post-war period had this set – *Left Hand, Right Hand, The Scarlet Tree* ... people who could barely have heard of the Sitwells, and whose lives were a million miles from the lives they led, their ancestors, the people they knew. My relatives had them. People who had almost no other books had them. It is a tribute to – well, to what? To a nifty piece of marketing by an early book club, I shouldn't wonder.

My year of reading from home may or may not include them, but it will have to have some books that are guaranteed to make me laugh and those are always just to hand, in the next room. I try to keep them together but one is always upstairs or downstairs or on the bedside table.

Humour in books is a very personal thing and not a subject about which to be superior. I am always overjoyed when my recommendation of P.G. Wodehouse is successful. Only recently, when I

recommended a friend start with *The Mating Season*, the next
e-mail I got from him was headed 'What ho!' But it ain't always so.
Another friend said he couldn't see the point of spending time with
such silly asses. You can't convert someone like that, you just have
to let it be.

People have occasionally asked me what book a teenage daughter
might read when she has grown out of children's books but not yet
grown into those for adults, and I often suggest one of the most
magical books on my shelves, as well as one of the funniest. It has
rarely failed.

Here's a clue.

> 'We are not moving to another Villa,' said Mother firmly. 'I've made
> up my mind about that.'
>
> She straightened her spectacles, gave Larry a defiant glare, and
> strutted off towards the kitchen, registering determination in every
> inch.

> PART TWO
> The new villa was enormous …

*My Family and Other Animals* never fails. It is one of the very few
books whose television adaptation was exactly right. So often the
plot may be there, and some pretty pictures, but the language, the
style, is missing, and a casting director's idea of a Dickens or
George Eliot character is rarely like mine. But this they got right.
Hannah Gordon *was* Mrs Durrell, Brian Blessed *was* Spiro …

It is a wonderful story, and a true one, about the springtime of
Gerald's life when he and his family 'fled from the gloom of the

English summer like a flock of migrating swallows' to the magical island of Corfu. The family are the heart of the book but into their dotty, squabbling, variegated net are drawn others, mainly Corfiots as well as Gerry's menagerie of odd creatures from odd sources, including a vicious gull given to him by a convict on parole, a young Scops owl rescued from an olive tree, stray dogs called Widdle and Puke, and two magpies always known as magenpies.Mother is the lynchpin of the family, gifted cook and gardener, tolerant and vague, forever deciding where she wants to be buried, forever teetering on the verge of insolvency. Gerry has the animals, Leslie hunts, Margo cares for her person, her clothes and keeping out of the sun, and Larry, of course, writes. The humour is far more than just a series of jokes, it arises from the characters and the situations. And Durrell writes so beautifully, especially of summer nights drenched in moonlight, wine, cicadas and the gentle wash of the sea, that he makes you want to fly off there too, like the family of migrating swallows. Actually, we once did, to a villa almost on a beach round the headland from the White House in which the last part of the book is set. I read the book again, sitting in the shade overlooking the emerald and turquoise sea so that my memories are somehow interwoven with Durrell's – and you can't beat that.

If the best books of humour emerge from characters and situations, the ones I always return to make me cry as well as laugh and how perfectly balanced are laughter and sadness in Nancy Mitford's *The Pursuit of Love*. I know it almost by heart, and hardly even need to fetch it from the shelf in the next room – know Davy telling Uncle Matthew that all the rare stones in the passage are diseased, and Uncle Matthew sobbing over his gramophone; know Linda, whose heart was so tender she could be made to cry for a lonely matchbox; know them all and never fail to laugh and cry alternately. But not every book that used to be funny goes on being so. It is rather chastening and I don't understand what happens. It happens to the reader not the book, of course; the book does not change. But somehow, what seemed hilarious can fall flat. I re-read *Three Men in a Boat* recently and it wasn't funny at all – well, the bit where they get lost in Hampton Court Maze was, though not quite as funny as it used to be. *The Diary of a Nobody* is no longer funny either, apart from the chapter in which they paint the bath red. Funny-ish. Why?

But P.G. Wodehouse never lets me down and it is only a question of whether I feel like Jeeves or Lord Emsworth. As Evelyn Waugh said, 'Mr Wodehouse's idyllic world will never stale.' It is timeless and the set pieces are magnificent – perhaps the scene of the village concert party (*The Mating Season*) or Gussie Fink-Nottle's speech at the school prize-giving (*Right Ho, Jeeves*) get the top marks but others might disagree.

The point about every single book that I re-read in order to laugh is that every one is so much more than funny because the authors write so well. Wodehouse uses the English language to perfection, Durrell evokes scenes so wonderfully, Nancy Mitford's prose is so elegant, so arch. One could learn to write from any of them and I wish more people would. No matter what the genre, good writing always tells. Crime novels? Look at Raymond Chandler, master of style. Spy novels? How many do you know who write as well as le Carré? Style wins every, every time.

# Amis, Père et Fils

THERE IS A very good reason why Elizabeth Jane Howard's novels are sitting on a shelf next to a couple of cookery books by Elizabeth David, and that is because of an association between the two of them in my past which goes back to 1961. I have never cooked from Elizabeth David's recipes but I have sometimes read her for the way she describes places associated with eating – the Mediterranean, the countryside of France.

In 1961, when my first book was published, I was sent off to Manchester to do an afternoon books programme which was fronted by a rising star of television called Brian Redhead, who later became a much-loved prop and stay of Radio 4's *Today* programme. Back then, a younger and more streamlined Brian ran a bright and lively TV series in which not only did he interview authors in the usual way, but had Elizabeth Jane Howard in a regular new-books review slot. So off I went on, believe it or not, the *sleeper* train to Manchester Piccadilly from London – I hardly believe it myself. Sleeper trains are the most romantic form of travel in the world, far more so than cruise ships once the epitome of romantic travel. I have taken sleepers across Europe and there is nothing, nothing in the world so exciting as waking in the night, drawing up the blind and finding oneself in the small hours at some remote mountain village station, where a couple of porters are smoking and watching the milk churns being loaded. 'Domodossola' says the sign. And the station is lit by a strange, dim light. It is a Graham Greene scene, or one out of an early Orson Welles movie, with someone sinister in a mac and trilby standing in the shadows, waiting, watching. Three hours later, wake again, and the blind snaps up to show Lake Montreux outside your window and children get on to the train for a few stops to school carrying bags of books – and skis. But this time it was only Manchester after all, in the company of Katharine Whitehorn, Elizabeth David and Elizabeth Jane Howard, grand-seeming ladies all, and terribly grown-up beside a student in a Marks & Spencer V-necked sweater. Elizabeth Jane was very kind about my book, and then I talked about student-cooking-on-a-gas-ring, with Katharine, who had written a book about just that, and Elizabeth David, who had not. She was a prickly lady, difficult to talk to, and she turned up her nose at everything on offer at lunchtime in the BBC canteen. Well, anybody might, but in those days I babysat for Arnold Wesker's children which made me an Aldermaston-marching sort of student who stood outside the college gates with placards about feeding Africa, so posh ladies being sniffy about the food that was set before them was never going to impress. I understand it all now, of course, and yes, the canteen lunch was awful and Mrs David had a pre-war and very refined palate and was one of the great cooks of her day. All the same, I still half-think she could have found some cheese and biscuits and an apple to eat.

Elizabeth Jane Howard was a fine cook, too, as I later discovered. She was extremely kind and encouraging to a starter-novelist and one never forgets that sort of generosity. I was lucky. I don't remember anyone, however eminent, who was not kind and encouraging. W.H. Auden, face creased like a map, was holding court to a circle of the great and the good one evening at the Snows. I had studied his poems for A level and it so happened that now, in my second year at King's, I was writing an essay about them. I told him so. In a trice, he had taken my hand, pulled me down to sit on the floor beside him and asked if there was anything he could help with. I remember my tongue cleaving to the roof of my mouth, I remember him blowing cigarette smoke all over me as he asked me, in his Anglo-American drawl, if there were any of his poems I found difficult to understand. I managed to name one. He sat back, narrowed his eyes, and expounded and I tried desperately to retain his words, wished I had brought a notebook, longed to follow his explanation. But it was generous, especially when important people, brought there to meet him, stood waiting by. Perhaps he preferred the company of a tongue-tied undergraduate to the literati after all.

It was in that same drawing room that I next bumped into Elizabeth Jane Howard, by then newly, and scandalously, married to Kingsley Amis. They dazzled everyone in the room: the beautiful people, the glamorous centre of attention. I met Kingsley, with whose handsomeness and charm I naturally fell in love. I had not read *Lucky Jim*, but thank goodness omitted to say so and borrowed a copy the following day. I never gave it back and it is here still, a battered old Penguin, and a novel I have never really found as funny as I know I should. I seemed to admire Kingsley's novels alternately – one on, one off – and *Lucky Jim* was off. I think, perhaps, it is a book for as well as about young men. At any rate, a lot of my male fellow students went about with copies, laughing heartily and quoting bits at one another, and none of the women did.

I last met him when he came in to be interviewed for *Bookshelf*, about his Booker-prize-winning novel *The Old Devils*. It was a deserved winner, a desperately moving, revealing novel which casts a great shadow because in it Kingsley revealed so much of himself and his terrors. It has a gravity and a strange dignity which the lighter comedies he wrote seem to lack – though he wrote nothing, nothing at all, which did not have its darker side.

By the time of our interview, drink had begun to take its toll, on his looks and his mental focus, but he was still grand company, still handsome beneath the ravages of whisky and misery, and he still had enormous charm. I don't think he actually rated women very much, yet like all such men he attracted them. I was extremely fond of him. And, whatever his son thinks to the contrary, he was enormously proud of Martin – I heard him say so in a way which was entirely genuine. Most of Kingsley Amis's novels are here next to most of Martin's. They sit well together. I have just been trying and failing yet again with *Lucky Jim*, and I think that must be the last time so I have taken down my favourite of his son's, *London Fields* and *Money*, to read one after another, before I go back, because it's a natural move to make, to Elizabeth Jane Howard's early novels. I do wish someone would re-publish them and with a bit of a fanfare, too. With books like *Something in Disguise*, *After Julius* and *The Sea Change* she became one of the best women novelists of the post-war years, with a powerful insight into human motivation and the underlying subtleties and complexities of apparently straight-forward relationships. She is especially good at depicting family entanglements and she writes so well, describes the world so vividly. I learned a lot about the art and craft of writing from those books, now undeservedly out of print.

# Never Got Around to It, Don't Like the Look of It, Couldn't Get Beyond Page Ten

## and Other Poor Excuses

THERE IS NO REASON why most of the books I own but have never actually read should be more or less in one place. They just are. Maybe they quietly gravitated into the sitting room one by one, to sob and huddle together for warmth.

A few years ago, Pierre Bayard wrote a book called *How to Talk about Books You Haven't Read*. I haven't read it, but I do wonder why people should actually want to do this. I daresay it's all tongue-in-cheek. Italo Calvino is reassuring about this whole subject in his masterly essay *Why Read the Classics?*

We need only observe that, however vast any person's basic reading may be, there still remain an enormous number of fundamental works he has not read. Let alone the non-fundamental ones.

From time to time, lists pop up on the books pages of newspapers. One hundred books nobody has ever read. Fifty books nobody ever finished reading. Ten books you can safely ignore. Well, they have to fill the pages. The trouble with so many of these lists is that they are a peg on which to hang a sneer, besides always, always listing the same books. Here we go, with my eyes shut … Proust, *Ulysses, War and Peace, Moby Dick, The Magic Mountain* …

The implication always seems to be that nobody can read them, everybody thinks they're boring and pointless, ergo, they must be boring and pointless, let's take these damn books down a peg or two.

But if one, just one, person has seen the point of them, has found them rich and life-changing enough to have earned the title of classic, which all of the above are, then their existence is justified and the fault is not in the books but in ourselves. Proust. Yes, I have made many an effort with Proust's *A La Recherche du Temps Perdu*, determined not to be one of those who list it, along with *War and Peace* and *Ulysses*, as one of their Unreadables. I have obeyed plenty of instructions as to how to read Proust. 'Race through it from first page to last, to get the hang of it; then go back and re-read it more carefully.' 'Take a volume, any volume, and start from there, don't feel you have to begin at Volume One.' 'Read about Proust first, then read the novel.' I have read *The Year of Reading Proust* by Phyllis Rose, and Alain de Botton's marvellously enlightening, engaging, thought-provoking *How Proust Can Change Your Life*. And both volumes of George Painter's *Biography*. I have even, foolishly, tried reading him in French. But the secret of Proust himself and his great novel continue to elude me. It is clearly me, not him – or rather, as with so many books, the combination of me/him, which separates rather than mixing smoothly.

Nor can I read *Ulysses*, though Stephen Fry, cleverer and better read than anyone I know, swears by it. He told me that it was just a question of diving in and swimming fast. Not for me it wasn't, I drowned. But I will go to the gallows to uphold the right of *Ulysses* to be called a classic.

The books I own but have not yet read are not all classics, not by a long chalk, though I see that *The Magic Mountain* is lurking there. So are the complete works of Scott, *Westward Ho!*, Mrs Gaskell's *North and South* and George Eliot's *Romola*. But, strangely, here is Julian Barnes' *Staring at the Sun* which is odd, given how often I have read his *Flaubert's Parrot*. I have actually read the whole of Henry James's *The Golden Bowl* and *The Ambassadors*, which count as 11 on the difficulty scale of 1–10, yet here, to my shame, I find the one everybody else has read and says is his finest, *The Portrait of a Lady*, and I haven't read that. Why? I have no idea. I have fallen into the impulse-buy temptation with a good many books that have found their way on to these shelves but remained unread. Here is *The Wall Jumper* by Peter Schneider, a Penguin Modern Classic I see, with a quote from Ian McEwan telling me it is a wonderful novel, and I daresay I will agree with him when I read it. Here is *The Great Gatsby* which my daughter loves more than any other book (bar Patrick McGrath's *Asylum*) and which she cannot believe I have never read. But then I cannot believe she has never read *Animal Farm* and, what is more, plans never to read it out of sheer cussedness. I don't *not* read books out of cussedness. That is not the reason why I haven't read any other book by Orwell except *Animal Farm*. I look at Orwell there, unopened, unsullied. I pick up *Down and Out in Paris and London*, *Keep the Aspidistra Flying* and *1984* and read the blurbs and even open the damn things, but a terrible miasma of tedium veils my eyes and I put them back on the shelf. Not Orwell. Me. It is always us, never the book, or almost never. (With Barbara Cartland, it is the book.)

Here is *Steppenwolf*, here is *Gormenghast*. Perhaps it's something to do with the titles? I can't swallow them whole.

But it is not only older books which shiver together, unread, unloved. Here are three books by Terry Pratchett, and I really have tried but it's no good … stories of wee small men … I can't. I bought several to see if they were any different but they're not. It scarcely matters. Terry Pratchett can do without me, so can every other fantasy writer and historical novelist who ever wrote, as can Linwood Barclay and Sadie Jones, Kate Morton, Julia Gregson, Khaled Hosseini … (You see the power of Richard and Judy? I buy them, I buy them, and that's that; I never read them. Another good reason for having a year of not buying a single new book.) Books I have never read but still might are on one side of the room. A lot of books I have read but will almost certainly never read again seem to have gathered on the other. It all happened of its own accord, by stealth, at night. I certainly did not make these volume arrangements.

I will never re-read most of the terminally suicidal novels by Jean Rhys though her masterpiece, *Wide Sargasso Sea*, is never far away. I will never re-read Anthony Powell, Dick Francis, Mary Renault or the only volume of science fiction I have ever finished, *The Voyage to Arcturus*, even though I see that Philip Pullman admires it. I read it because I was told it was the sci-fi novel people who hated sci-fi novels loved. Some of them may.

Oh but look, I almost pulled out John Wyndham. What are his books doing on the never-to-be-re-read shelf? *The Day of the Triffids. The Midwich Cuckoos. The Chrysalids.* They are sci-fi. Or are they? Horror? In a way. Fantasy? Kind of. Frightening? You bet.

I have brought them upstairs and put them on the bedside table where there is always something scary sitting waiting to be read in the wee small hours.

# A Little List

A SPECIAL RELATIONSHIP is formed with books that have been on our shelves for years without being read. They become known in a strange way, perhaps because we have read a lot about them, or they are books that are part of our overall heritage. I think I know a lot about *Don Quixote*. I *do* know a lot about *Don Quixote*. I have just never read it. I doubt if I ever will. But I know what people mean when they talk about tilting at windmills; I recognise a drawing of Quixote and Sancho Panza. I believe Cervantes to be a great European writer. Why do I believe that? What possible grounds have I for believing it? Other people's opinions, the fact that it has an honourable and permanent place in the canon? So, *Don Quixote* has an honourable, permanent place on my shelves. It would be wrong to get rid of it and, besides, I should miss its red leather binding.

Some books I have not read are here temporarily – paperbacks bought on a whim, novels someone has persuaded me I will love but I know, by one glance at the cover and blurb, that I will not.

They will not stick around. They are waiting for the next consignment to the charity bookshop.

On the other hand, some not-read books are just waiting for their time to come. It will, it will, perhaps when I am very old, or have an illness that requires me to stay in bed for days but that does not make me feel too rotten to read. Perhaps I will take one on a train. I read a lot on trains and if I were to have one book, and that a book I have not yet read, then I would have to read it.

There are books I have not read which I know I will love; and I'll be amazed and distressed when I *do* get round to them that I did not allow them to enrich my life years ago. *Tom Jones* falls into this category. I managed to slither by Fielding quite successfully at university but I should not die without having read him. Or *Villette*. Or *Le Morte d'Arthur*. Or Arthur Ransome.

Some people take a pride in not having read a particular book, as if the not-reading were some sort of achievement, a badge to be worn with pride like the one worn by those who do not have a television, or, like dons we knew in Oxford, 'We do have a set, but only in black and white and we keep it in a cupboard.'

On a bright, brave May day, with the hawthorn blossom creaming all over the hedgerows and the swallows swooping over the chimney pots, I went looking for books I have not read. I was shocked by how many I found here. These, for instance:

*The Bonfire of the Vanities.* Tom Wolfe.
'A day-glo Dickens.' *The Sunday Times*. It is all about decadent New York and money in the 1980s. *The Washington Post* tells me it is 'a superb human comedy'. So why have I never read this book?

*Precious Bane*. Mary Webb.
I've read *Cold Comfort Farm* enough times and that was based on this, so maybe I don't need to read this.

*Deceived with Kindness*. Angelica Garnett.
Probably the only Bloomsbury book I haven't read. Which is odd. I must have been saving it up like the last Rolo.

*Eucalyptus*. Murray Bail.
Someone told me that this was a great novel so I bought it, but then discovered that it was a great Australian novel so I put it away. I find it difficult to get to grips with Australian novels. Difficult, but not impossible.

*Buddenbrooks*. Thomas Mann.
I want to read this. I mean to read this. I really do.

*The House on the Borderland*. William Hope Hodgson.
Horror story. I find you have to be in the right mood for these.

*The Little Prince (Le Petit Prince)*. Antoine de Saint-Exupéry
I don't understand how I can have not read it.

*Romola*. George Eliot.
I do understand how I can have not read it.

There is a wonderful essay called 'Books Unread' by Thomas Wentworth Higginson, the great American abolitionist. It appeared first in *The Atlantic Monthly* in 1904.

The only knowledge that involves no burden lies … in the books that are left unread. I mean, those which remain undisturbed, long and perhaps forever, on a student's bookshelves; books for which he possibly economized and for which he went without his dinner; books on whose back his eyes have rested a thousand times, tenderly and almost lovingly, until he has perhaps forgotten the very language in which they are written. He has never read them, yet during these years there has never been a day when he would have sold them; they are a part of his youth. In dreams he turns to them … He awakens, and whole shelves of his library are, as it were, like fair maidens who smiled on him in their youth and then passed away. Under different circumstances, who knows but one of them might have been his? As it is, they have grown old apart from him; yet for him they retain their charms.

Wordsworth says, 'Dreams, books, are each a world.'

And the books unread mingle with the dreams and unite the charm of both … Yet if a book is to be left unread at last, the fault must ultimately rest with the author, even as the brilliant Lady Eastlake complained, when she wrote of modern English novelists:

Things are written now to be read once and no more; that is, they are read as often as they deserve. A book in old times took five years to write and was read five hundred times by five hundred people. Now it is written in three months and read once by five hundred thousand people. That's the proper proportion.

I might one day move all the unread books to one room and see how far they stretch along the shelves. How much should I allow, out of my year of reading from home, for *Don Quixote? The Bonfire of the Vanities?* Arthur Ransome? *Romola?* …

# Things that Fall out of Books

BILLS, PAID OR UNPAID. Receipts. Picture postcards. Here is a copy of Graham Greene's *The Third Man* out of which falls a postcard from Dirk Bogarde:

'Dear Susan, I have just spent a happy afternoon at Penguin Books with my editor, drinking peppermint tea and trying to think of alternative words for "penis".'

A receipt for a car service dated 1983 somehow found its way into a spare copy of *The Book of Common Prayer*. The Order of Service for the funeral of a dear, good friend is in my best copy of T.S. Eliot's *Four Quartets*. I know why that is there – this friend knew the *Quartets* by heart and understood them as well as anyone I ever met so I slipped the funeral sheet in a place he would have liked it to be. Old letters, old shopping lists. 'Phone chimney sweep.' 'Pay gardener.' Old phone numbers.

And here, out of a work of genius, falls a handmade Christmas card from its author, drawn by herself. It is made out of pale blue folded paper and glued on to the front is an ink drawing of a small boy in long shorts, using a stool to reach a book from a high shelf. It is done in ink and the line is confident and simple, yet the little there actually is on the page somehow reveals an awful lot more, like Eliot's 'unheard music, hidden in the shrubbery'.

How absolutely right and all of a piece with the book out of which it fell and with the rest of her work.

'Dear Susan

A Very Happy Christmas and New Year, With best wishes from Penelope.'

The novel is *The Blue Flower*. The Penelope is Fitzgerald.

I have never, ever understood why it did not win every prize extant but prize-judging is a law unto itself, as it were. I have been on the panels of many, and never once have things gone as might have been predicted. I was a judge for a major prize the year *The Blue Flower* was entered and I have never tried so hard to convince others of anything as I did that this was a rare, a great, novel whose like we might none of us see again. It was not that my fellow judges were wilfully determined not to agree, or had anything whatsoever against Penelope Fitzgerald – for who could? They simply could not see it. They saw something pleasing, short. Slight. That was the word I heard again and again. 'Slight'. I think I sweated blood, but to no purpose.

'Slight'. Slight? SLIGHT?

*The Blue Flower* is a masterpiece. It is the most extraordinary book, and half of it is in invisible writing, so much is there that is not there, so much lies below the surface, so much is left unsaid and yet is redolent and rich with meaning. Fitzgerald manages that quite remarkable feat – she simply walks into another world, one of several hundred years ago in another country, and takes up the story, moving among the characters as if she had known them all her life, and so the reader does so, too. Her prose style, like the line of the drawing on the Christmas card, is so clear, clean and simple, and yet so full of meaning. She was a past-mistress of dialogue, she knew how to make places taste and smell, knew what they sounded like. She saw into other people's minds and hearts with complete empathy. It is my favourite of all her books and it is gratifying that slowly, slowly over a decade or so, *The Blue Flower* is being recognised and lauded as indeed a novel of genius, and a masterpiece. During the celebrations for the fortieth anniversary of the Booker Prize, time and again it was mentioned with bewilderment as 'the one that got away'. I hope that she knew her value. She was a shy and modest woman and yet underneath that exterior, I think she did realise her own worth, though she would never have been vain about it.

When I started a quarterly magazine called *Books and Company*, I asked Penelope to write for the first issue. She replied that she would and her letter began with characteristic generosity. 'Please allow me to congratulate you on starting a magazine about books and the enjoyment of reading – something to be wholeheartedly supported.' Over the next few weeks we exchanged a few letters about her piece – it was on Sarah Orne Jewett's book *The Country of the Pointed Firs* – and in one of them she mentioned the pleasure of having grandchildren, in a phrase I will remember to my dying day.

'It is such a joy,' she writes, 'to have someone who wishes to sit with you on a sofa and *listen to a watch tick*.'

# It Ain't Broke

THE BOOK, THAT IS. I know because I just went round the house looking for something to read, and on the way I reassured myself that as the book ain't broke around here, I do not propose to fix it with an electronic reader. Yes, let's use the whole word. Let's tell it like it is. Electronic reader. Something monotonous-looking and made of plastic, is grey and has a screen. Maybe that's the problem. It's the screen that worries us. Cinema screen, television screen, computer screen, windscreen. Ah yes, windscreen. A friend of mine used to say that all the problems of the modern world – all of them – could be laid at the door of the internal combustion engine. Well, I blame the screen, too, and although I am not about to give up my own internal combustion engine or what was, for a nanosecond, called the goggle-box, I will stick to paper and print and pages for reading books. If it ain't broke. Of course, someone wants to persuade us that it is so that they can sell us their device. 'Twas ever thus.

But on my travels round the house in search of just the right book for tonight, I passed so many reasons why the book works as well as it ever did. Tall thin reasons. Huge, heavy, illustrated ones. Small, neat, square hardbacks and pocket-sized paperbacks. Reasons with drawings, with photographs, with colour. Shiny ones. Matt ones. Cheap ones, expensive ones. Chunky ones. Some smell new, of paper and almost, but not quite, fresh ink. Some smell musty. Some have the signature of the author. A few are dedicated by the author, either to one of us or to someone unknown and long dead. Some have pencil marks scribbled in the margin – my own student hand in the Robinson edition of Chaucer, my daughter's schoolgirl hand in *A Tale of Two Cities*, my aunt's in *Middlemarch* and *Jane Eyre*, which she used to teach fifty years ago. Here is a book I bought second- or third-hand which has 'To Patrick, remembering our days at the seminary' written in the front. Here is *Vanity Fair*, with 'F...k Off' in red pen on page 146 (not in my writing).

No one will sign an electronic book, no one can annotate in the margin, no one can leave a love letter casually between the leaves. It is true that if I had no books but only a small, flat, grey hand-held electronic device, I would only need a very small house and how tidy that would be with just the small, flat, grey ...

But I was looking for a book. I have no option but to find one here, in this house, for this is my year of reading from home and suddenly there is nothing, absolutely nothing, I want to take down and open, to read or re-read. I don't think the fault lies in the books; the feeling applies to the wardrobe (nothing I want to wear), or the full larder (nothing I want to eat). I daresay very rich people with the private jet standing by have the same problem – nowhere they want to go.

I have even been to the very top of the house, though more for the exercise than in the hope of finding a book I wanted to read because the room that lies beyond the last flight of stairs is the domain of the SP (Shakespeare Professor), and entirely given over to Shakespeare, with a side-serving of his contemporaries. I don't want to read *Hamlet*, or *Cymbeline*, or a learned scholar on the Comedies, Tragedies or Histories. Or I don't think I do until I get up there and start browsing. Here is E.M.W. Tillyard's *The Elizabethan World Picture*, which first fired me with an enthusiasm for that age when I was doing A-level history on the Tudors. That tempts me, and so does Conyers Read's great biography *Mr. Secretary Cecil and Queen Elizabeth* and one of the academic Shakespeare books – Anne Barton's *Shakespeare and the Idea of the Play* – that once sent me off on reading-journeys in all manner of exciting directions. Here is a row of books by my old Professor at King's, Geoffrey Bullough – *Narrative and Dramatic Sources of Shakespeare*, eight heavy uniform volumes and a major life's work of scholarship. Professor Bullough had become very eminent by the time he was teaching my generation of students but took as much trouble with us as he might with a group of his peers, always courteous, always happy to go over something again, always encouraging, a shining example to all those at the top of their game who still have to, and should, spend some of their precious time teaching beginners.

But *Narrative and Dramatic Sources of Shakespeare* is not what even the SP would call 'a reading book'. I come back down to the small bookcase in the alcove outside my bedroom, which contains old favourites, books I often want to re-read, comfort books, and one or two which have never quite found their right place, so are resting on the branches here until they migrate to a more permanent home.

'I'll tidy your books for you,' a so-called friend said, coming to the house and declaring that she did not know how I stood it. 'I'll categorise them and re-organise them so that you'll never lose one again.'

How can she not understand that if I let her do such a terrible thing as organise my books, I would never find what I was looking for again? Worse, there would never be any wonderful surprises, as I look for X and Y but, *mirabile dictu*, find Z, which I thought I had lost years ago. Never the marvellous juxtaposition of a biography of Marilyn Monroe next to *Charlie and the Chocolate Factory*.

I was still looking for a book to read. I did not want anything too ephemeral, was not in the mood for humour, needed something sober but not sombre, familiar but with plenty of meat left on the bone. I was determined to make an effort, too, not plump for *The Thirty-Nine Steps* yet again. I have come downstairs again, to the small room that has changed its purpose in life several times since we came to this house, from younger daughter's bedroom, to office, to general purpose 'book and stationery storage room'. I have several times made plans to change it again, into a small reading room, because it is at the front of the house, with a wonderful view. The trouble is that the window is set very slightly too high, so that you cannot see the view when seated; I once evolved a second, or side-plan, to have a carpenter raise the floor up by building a low platform. I have not carried this plan out because the front of the house leans slightly to the left and the floors, of course, with it, making the construction of a wooden platform slightly more complicated than first measurements allow. It can be done, of course. Anything can be done. But it has been relegated to a back-burner job in terms of the household economy – there always seems to be some boiler-repair or dangerous tree-felling or car-brakes job which is more urgent.

The little room has as strange an assortment of books as any other in the house – Medieval Monastic history cheek by jowl with 400 Ladybird Books. Spring makes promises in March. There are a few warm days when it is good to bask in the early sun, but through glass, sitting with a book on the windowseat. When I look up, I see a faint wash of pale green across the poplars and the blue crocuses make fairy rings round the base of the acer trees. Daffodils tremble in the March winds. Walking out is all very fine but sitting to read is still better done indoors.

And here, at last, I find what I am looking for – a book to read. If ever I am in this restless and unsettled book-reading state, I know what will always satisfy, always interest me, always welcome me into the depths of its being. There are plenty of them in the house, some upstairs, some down, but I have found a row of them here, clustered together on the top of a high set of shelves, so that I need the step-stool to reach them.

What I have found are …

# … Diaries

PEPYS WROTE HIS DIARY in cypher. Did he intend that no one else should ever read it? Did the Elizabethan Simon Forman, who recorded his sexual exploits, also in code, write only for himself? I know one or two people who keep a diary. Some, they say, are simple accounts of everyday family life, of no interest to anyone else nor intended to be seen by others. They are interesting for the writer to look back on in ten or twenty years. 'What was I doing on this day in 1980? What did I wear for Mary's wedding? What was the weather like on Joe's twenty-first birthday?' If diaries like these are discovered in two hundred years' time they will be of interest to social historians, for it is the minutiae of ordinary lives which get lost far more easily than the records of great events, because people have thought them not worth recording.

There are a surprising number of other people's published diaries on my shelves and a few that were clearly written with an eye to posterity and publication – mainly by politicians. They are mainly pretty dull, too, though those of Alan Clark are the great exception. Was there ever a politician with more sexual charisma than Clark? Yet I have often thought that he didn't really like women, and I doubt if he ever loved a single one of the many, many he conquered, except his wife Jane. His diaries are riveting. He had the essential attribute for the great diarist, a clear eye which not only saw but saw through, spotting the giveaway expression, the tell-tale nervous tic, able to guess pretty accurately what went on behind a public mask. Most political diaries reveal so little of the diarist themselves that somehow, as a result, they do not reveal much about other people either. Clark knew and revealed himself – or I think he did – and was very aware of his own follies and failings, weaknesses and wickednesses. I wonder if he knew that his reader could thoroughly disapprove of almost everything he does and says, and most of what he stands for, and yet admire him – like him, even.

I met him when I was, rather inappropriately, making a BBC film for a series about Shakespeare, and the producer had rented Saltwood Castle, where he lived, as his father, Lord Clark of *Civilisation*, had lived before him. It's an oddly homely castle, not large enough to be intimidating, and it was a good, if slightly incongruous place to film a programme about *Othello*. There are always hanging-about times when making a film, and during one of them I went for a walk about and met Alan Clark – our host, as it were, unmistakeable, handsome in the craggy and cruel way that felled so many women, and, unlike his castle, pretty intimidating. He asked what I was doing. I said I was waiting for them to call me for the next shot. He asked how long that would be. I said I had no idea. It might be two minutes or half an hour.

'Bored?' he asked.

'Yes.'

'Go and count the tortoises.'

I'd noticed one or two but when I did as I was told I discovered dozens about the castle grounds, some still as stones and easy to mistake for one, some lumbering quietly along a path or across the grass. It was fun. I don't remember how many I counted but by the time I got back to report, Clark had disappeared anyway.

His diaries never fail to amuse, divert, interest, throw light on this or that and their author is good company – less intimidating than in real life, too.

The Reverend Francis Kilvert would not have been intimidating. Here is the hardback set of his diaries in three handsome volumes originally published by Jonathan Cape, dust wrappers intact and lurking in a small bookcase in a dark corner. It is there because the bookcase holds tall books, but then, so do others and Kilvert deserves a better home.

It seems likely that he wrote his diary with one eye on posterity, because it is so carefully composed and the descriptions of the country, the seasons, the weather, the daily round of a clergyman, are set down with an exactness and a poetic touch that are unusual in a very private diary. There is probably no better place to go, than these beautiful diaries, to discover the countryside of the Black Mountains and the life of the people there, in remote villages and farms, as it was in the nineteenth century. Much has changed there now, but the hills themselves have not and nor has the atmosphere in these places on the English–Welsh border – some find it spooky.

Kilvert was a fellow spirit with Lewis Carroll, another Victorian clergyman susceptible to the charms of little girls. He describes the beauty of a string of them, the bright eyes or the dark hair or the flashing glances, whom he saw as he walked for miles, visiting schools, farms, cottages. Once, he admits that he walked ten miles merely for a smile from one of them, with whom he was in love. How sad that he and Carroll would now be called paedophiles; they were innocent men both, and devoutly Christian. Neither would have harmed any child and their frustrations must have been immense.

Kilvert led an active social life among the local squirearchy, and gentry, too, as well as being a conscientious parish priest, and eventually he married, only to die of peritonitis a few weeks later.

I have found a great many riches over many years of reading his diaries, introduced to them as I was by their original editor, William Plomer. I borrowed something from Kilvert, too, for my novel *In the Springtime of the Year*, about a young woman whose beloved husband of a year is killed by a falling tree. When the person I had been going to marry died suddenly, and I wrote the novel as an act of both love and of catharsis, I derived a great deal of comfort from Kilvert, and his evocation of landscapes, of country ways and the Church's year soaks the book. Much of it was transmuted, as such things always are, but I borrowed directly from one scene he describes so wonderfully.

But now the customary beautiful Easter Eve idyll had fairly begun and people kept arriving from all parts with flowers to dress the graves. Children were coming from the town and from neighbouring villages with baskets of flowers and knives to cut holes in the turf. The roads were lovely with people coming and going and the churchyard a busy scene with women and children and a few men moving about among the tombstones and kneeling down beside the green mounds flowering the graves. I found a child wandering about the tombs looking for her father's grave. She had found her grandfather's and had already dressed it with flowers. The clerk was banking up and watering the green mounds not far off and I got him to come and show the child where the father's grave lay. He soon found it, for he knows almost every grave in the churchyard. And then I helped the child to dress the long narrow green mound with the flowers that remained in her basket …

More and more people kept coming into the churchyard as they finished their day's work. The sun went down in glory behind the dingle but still the work of love went on through the twilight and into the dusk until the moon rose full and splendid. The figures continued to move about among the graves and to bend over the green mounds in the calm clear moonlight and warm air of the balmy evening …

(Later) as I walked down the churchyard alone the decked graves had a strange effect in the moonlight and looked as if the people had lain down to sleep for the night out of doors, ready dressed to rise early on Easter morning.

The best way to know Kilvert and his world is to read the three volumes from beginning to end, chronologically, and then to dip in and out over the months and years, getting to know this shy, passionate, intelligent, sensitive, conscientious man and the people he served, the countryside he walked until he was familiar with it, in all its moods and seasons. I scarcely know of a better bedside book or a finer companion.

I cannot now remember how I first came to know William Plomer, poet, novelist, Kilvert's editor, publisher's editor, friend of

Leonard and Virginia Woolf, and librettist for the three church parables set to music by Benjamin Britten. But I remember him and many of our meetings, vividly. He was one of those people who probably showed a different persona to every friend, and he was full of contradictions which made up an enigmatic whole. He had led a wildly varied life, from his youth in South Africa onwards – but the most incongruous thing I know about him is that he edited several of Ian Fleming's early James Bond novels, when he worked for Jonathan Cape. Anyone less like Fleming, or Bond, or suited to the world of Bond, than William it would be hard to imagine, yet Fleming counted him as his close and most loyal friend and collaborator. William was a dapper man, rather formal, kind, shrewd, with a fund of excellent stories. All of that concealed a promiscuous homosexual, and one with a curious home life. He lived in a small bungalow in suburban Sussex, with a European wartime refugee who kept house, but he was frequently away, on Kilvert business – he was founder, leading light and President of the Kilvert Society for many years, he was a fine poet and he gave many public readings, he travelled abroad, he wrote, he lectured, he read, reported on and edited books for Cape, he reviewed.

He was often in London, where I had some jolly lunches with him at his favourite French restaurant off Leicester Square, Chez Solange. He was a generous host, enjoyed classic French cooking and once told me that he liked to push the boat out now and then because he ate 'rather frugally' at home. I grew extremely fond of him; he was a tactful and wise confidant, a fountain of sensible advice which was proffered but never imposed. His novels were interesting and perceptive and he portrayed women particularly well, but these have dated and it is as a poet that he deserves to be remembered (though I rather doubt if he is). But the many lovers of Kilvert owe him the greatest debt of all, for his dedication to editing, publishing and promoting the *Diary* far and wide. Without William Plomer we would not have the joy of Kilvert on our shelves at all.

I think the greatest satisfaction of reading published diaries is that of being admitted into other people's worlds, of living in their houses, knowing their friends, accompanying them on their travels – and at the same time being party to their views of it all. It is like plunging into the imaginary world of a novel and yet satisfying in a rather different way – one I have not yet quite managed to put my finger on. The other side of that coin, though, is a sense of being a voyeur and that is more troubling the closer the diarist's lifetime is to one's own. I do not feel an intruder into Kilvert's world because both he and those about whom he writes are so very far away, and all of them dead. And Kilvert is almost always gentle and generous in his portrayal of others, as his Christianity bade him be. There is the occasional sigh, the occasional ironic aside, but, in general, he is accepting and forgiving even as he portrays people so clearly – and that in itself is no mean feat. I have not found many other diarists of previous centuries of such interest, though the charms of Gilbert White's *Natural History of Selborne* are manifest. But they are specific. One reads White for his observation of the natural world, within and beyond his own garden, for the weather and the birds, the plants and the tortoise. Some people read Parson Wood-forde because they find lists of what someone in the eighteenth century ate and drank – a prodigious amount – of absorbing inter-est, which I do not. A dull diary, that one.

If a diarist chooses to make his own life and doings, reflections and reactions, public, that's up to him, but I do wonder how far it is acceptable to tell us about his friends and casual acquaintances while they are still alive, even more so when I discover in published pages accounts of people I myself have known (and indeed, sometimes do not recognise, so different is the person I have met from the one the diarist seems to have encountered).

I find volumes of diaries in almost every room. Here, snugly beside the complete novels of Graham Greene, is the paperback of *The Roy Strong Diaries*, which make good reading for two reasons. The first is that they are a clear record, not to say indictment, of the dreadful 1960s and 1970s, when the trades unions held such sway in this country, and Roy Strong, as Director first of the National Portrait Gallery and later of the V&A almost lost his health, strength and sanity in the war of attrition against them.

Otherwise, one reads Roy for gossip. Like so many people who have danced on the sidelines of Royal circles, he spills the beans about them with enthusiasm. I have noticed this in others, even in apparently very close friends of the Royals – they make the worst (or best, depending on your point of view) gossips about them, telling all sorts of tales out of school. No wonder the Royal Family really only trust one another. But aside from the froth and bubble of society, Roy Strong has one of the gifts of the great diarist – the knack of getting to the heart of a person, pinning them down on paper in a paragraph, of cutting out appearances and summing them up acutely. You have to trust that the diarist gets it right and the only way of being sure is to judge by a swift pen-portrait of someone you have actually known. Roy passes this test almost every time. Plenty of people have written about the London society hostess Pamela Hartwell – she crops up in many a diary. But Roy

Strong's summing up of her is brilliant, incisive, shrewd, affectionate but clear-eyed.

> When last we had lunch together shortly before Christmas she was
> as vibrant, strident, dominant and magnificent as ever … That she
> was an extraordinary woman there can be no doubt. Her problem
> lay in the fact that her intellect had never been trained … As a
> consequence, her life was one long explosion of misapplied and
> frustrated energy as she bulldozed her way first as a political hostess,
> then as the presiding deity of British couture, and latterly as a lady
> of art. The result was an eternal unfulfilled restlessness as she
> pursued first this path then that. This erratic progress was matched
> by her guest-list, which also speedily changed as people came on it
> and as quickly came off it. Politics, fashion and art fell beneath her
> chariot wheels but she never actually displayed any deep knowledge
> of any of them … So what was it about her that one found so com-
> pulsive? I think that it was her vitality and energy, which were on a
> terrific scale, and her appetite for people … Pam stood firmly in a
> line of descent back to the eighteenth century, that of a great hostess
> bringing people together. They intrigued her and she needled out of
> them all she could. Liking them certainly didn't enter into it. And
> she was never happy at anyone's party except her own.
>
> Once, she must have had some dress sense for she was the main-
> stay of post-war revived British couture. But for as long as I knew
> her she always wore violent-coloured rather ethnic dresses and vast
> clanking gobbets of artificial jewellery.

She could have come straight out of one of Trollope's political
novels.

I now realise that it is a diary that I have been looking for all over the house, a diary with a life round which numerous other lives, celebrated and obscure, revolve, a diary with an interesting diarist at its heart but one with whom I do not always see eye to eye. I do not need to like my diarist but I want to find their company stimulating. I have gathered up, from the highways and byways of various bookshelves in various rooms, two complete sets of diaries. I am going to read those again.

The *Diary* of James Lees-Milne has magnificent titles; as enticing as those of Diana Cooper's autobiographies, *The Rainbow Comes and Goes*, *Trumpets from the Steep* and *The Light of Common Day*; or of Osbert Sitwell – who would not want to read a memoir called *Laughter in the Next Room*?

Lees-Milne's most enticing titles are from Coleridge – *Caves of Ice*, *The Milk of Paradise*, *Holy Dread*, and here they are, hardback first editions laid in a row, above another row I have set out on the table, the complete diaries of Frances Partridge, whose titles are more pedestrian.

I have a problem with both these diarists, and it is exacerbated because I have read them both so many times, and always want to read them again, always want to re-enter their worlds, always find innumerable good companions there. Yet they trouble me. My own interest in them troubles me.

I selected two volumes of Frances Partridge's diary and started reading them again. The first thing that strikes me is her tenacious bravery and stoicism in carrying on living after the deaths of her husband and, three years later, her only son, Burgo. She questions her decision from time to time, discusses possible suicide, quite rationally, before rejecting it. She decides to live on (and, indeed, she was 104 when she died) in the hope that the meaning she finds in various aspects of life – friends, work, art, music, the intellect – will continue to give her reason for doing so. It seems that it did, and who could not salute her courage?

Yet there is the cold aura of Bloomsbury arrogance and lack of feeling about these diaries, a retailing and dissecting of the behaviour of close friends, and recounting of incidents which show them in a bad light, which repels. Partridge, like most of the Bloomsbury Group, was sure her way, the way of clear reason and the intellect, was the best, the superior, the only way to live and the downside of this is the scorn with which she dismisses those who found other ways. She holidays with Rosamond Lehmann, apparently with some enjoyment, yet makes her both look and sound a vacuous fool because of her belief in a God and an afterlife. It is all dismissed as 'Ros's spooks'.

I always turn to the Partridge diaries eagerly and read them with absorption, but I leave them feeling, for some of the time at least, that I should not have been reading them at all. Occasionally, I answer them back. 'No, no, you've got it quite wrong. X was not like that.' And if X was not like that, what about all the others? Do I take her word for it?

I have to take James Lees-Milne's word for it on the subject of himself, for that is really the point of reading the volumes, published with such alacrity during his lifetime. Yes, they are a record of his times, and he is a valuable recorder of the workings of the National Trust during an important period of its existence, as Roy Strong is of the V&A. These are the diaries of a name-dropper and they irritate, as every page is littered with symbols pointing to explanatory footnotes, which interrupt the flow. Lees-Milne is the snob to end all snobs, vain, intemperate and intolerant, self-regarding and self-important. But his saving grace is that he knows it and bewails his own follies and foibles in such a manner as to disarm all criticism. I came to love him as I read his diaries for the first time because such a clear-eyed and unforgiving view of self is so rare and entirely refreshing.

Here are the diaries, on the table – I could spend my year reading from home on diaries alone. And if I had to pick one? Virginia Woolf's *A Writer's Diary* is never away from my bedside table, well worn, much-loved, a constant inspiration. It was by way of that single volume, extracted by Leonard from her many volumes of diaries, that I was led to her novels, and so to the woman I have loved and admired and been fascinated by for fifty years. And still am, still am. But I know the book so well, have read the print off its pages for so long, that it has become part of me. I must choose something else. Simon Gray's diaries, then? A late love, these, and diaries like no other; specific, funny, mordant, heartening and saddening at the same time. His last, *Coda*, about his final year after diagnosis of lung cancer, is almost unbearable to read, so candid is he about his feelings and fears, so wonderfully, generously revealing of himself, for our edification and delight, and even comfort. The first, *The Smoking Diaries*, might be the one to read this year so I've picked it up and as I do so, of course, I wish for the thousandth time that we had met. We almost did. I kept saying that we would, to Victoria, his wife, promising to meet up when I was in London with an hour free for coffee. For anything. Somehow, I never did, somehow, it was always going to be after Christmas, or when you get back from Barbados, or when I've finished my book or …

Simon sent me a copy of the third diary, *The Last Cigarette*, with a friendly inscription. And then he died and I still hadn't made the extra effort, found the day in London with an hour to spare.

Do it now. I thought I'd learned that lesson a long time ago.

In the end, I turn from all of them to a single fat paperback.

Like Proust, like James Joyce, like *War and Peace*, the novels of Sir Walter Scott appear on most lists of Unreadable Books, though once they were as popular as the novels of Dickens, and every self-respecting middle-class home had a complete set of them.

So it was with various failed attempts to get through *Rob Roy* or *The Heart of Midlothian* in mind that I greeted a copy of *The Journal of Sir Walter Scott* when it arrived on my doorstep, sent by the friend who edited it, Eric Anderson. I glanced at the book and glanced away, and for some months it sat on the low table in the drawing room, resolutely closed. Then, one grey afternoon in February, I sat in the armchair, thinking to read and, before I had quite decided what I would read, picked up that book.

Two hours later, I was delightedly absorbed in the journal and making the acquaintance of a man I liked, admired and found the most wonderful company in the world. Never mind the novels, read the man himself, who speaks plainly yet whose powers of description are mighty, whose great spirit, courage, uprightness, generosity and warm humour leap out of these pages. He almost persuades me to enjoy Jane Austen, his praise of her is so high-hearted and generous.

That young lady had a talent for describing the involvements and feelings and characters of ordinary life which is to me the most wonderful I ever met with. The Big Bow-wow strain I can do myself like any now going, but the exquisite touch which renders ordinary common-place things and characters interesting from the truth of the description and the sentiment is denied to me. What a pity such a gifted creature died so early.

But not being able to enjoy Jane Austen is a subject for another day. I have found my book and as it is a cold, grey afternoon, I will light a fire in the drawing room, and begin again *The Journal of Sir Walter Scott*.

# 'One Half of the World Cannot Understand the Pleasures of the Other.'

AS JANE AUSTEN says. I knew she would understand. But I need to get to grips with this problem because there could scarcely be a more key author for me to miss the point of than Austen. And I do miss the point, almost entirely.

I married into a handsome Oxford set of the novels, and here they are, pale-grey bindings, fine creamy paper, elegant font, well-designed on the page, weighing nicely in the hand, so I cannot complain of having to read old paperbacks or that it is all the fault of the tiny print in the small World's Classics edition.

I cannot blame school or the exam system either, for Austen was never a set book, and I skimmed with a light foot over the early nineteenth-century novel when I was reading for my degree, leaving barely a trace of my passing. I have never had to dissect and analyse and compose an essay on Austen, I have simply had to enjoy her. And I don't.

Worse. I am bored by Jane Austen.

There now, I've said it.

It is not that I simply cannot get through the novels – they do not join Proust or James Joyce on the Impossible shelf. I have read them all, several times, and if I am obliged to read one again it will be *Northanger Abbey*, which I have enjoyed tolerably well. But that is surely not enough. Look at the Janeites, look at the widespread ability to quote whole paragraphs, whole chunks of dialogue, out of pure love. Look, even, at the huge success of every film and television adaptation. Though I am not a fan of the Classic Serial, many have been led to great books via that route.

My younger daughter learned to love Jane Austen from the BBC television adaptation starring Colin Firth and a clutch of other fine actors. She watched it so many times that she knew it by heart and could hardly be deterred from reciting entire scenes for our entertainment, until, like Mary, she had delighted us long enough. I have watched it several times with her and although Firth is not my idea of Darcy, many of the other characters were perfectly cast. Alison Steadman and Benjamin Whitrow as the Bennets could not be faulted.

Perhaps the nineteenth century, whose style of dress and architecture, design and manners, I find cold and distancing, is to blame for my inability to appreciate Austen, whose cool, ironic style is somehow all of a piece with that formality and porcelain veneer. Yes, there is wit, there are acute asides, there is a sharpness of observation and judgement, but I never feel empathy with, or closeness to, an Austen character. That may be because their author, their creator, discourages intimacy. She is herself politely distant, keeps me at arm's length, is too private and reserved. I cannot get to know her and if I cannot do that, how can I like her or be interested in what she has to tell me about her characters and their situations? It is all too patterned, too much like one of those boring formal dances they performed, all too stylised. I want someone to break out of the elegant little drawing-room circle and go mad. Lydia Bennet almost does it.

If every other book in the house was stolen and I had to spend my year reading Jane Austen only, I would either become an ardent fan, after suddenly getting the point, or I would be the one to go mad.

Then I remember what an English-teacher at school told me long ago when I confessed to her – a passionate and knowledgeable Janeite – that I could not get along with the novels. 'Nor could I at your age. Don't worry. She will seem very different when you grow up.'

So I put the Oxford complete novels back on the shelf, to wait until then.

# 'Life is a Handful of Short Stories Pretending to be a Novel.'

I JOTTED THAT anonymous quotation down on the inside of a notebook some time ago. So many of those neat little matchbox quotes seem profound at first acquaintance but rapidly lose their profundity the more carefully you analyse them. That one is not especially profound but it is fairly true. About life, though, not about the short story. It was William Faulkner, that novelist of the Deep South whose books I so loved when I was twenty and cannot now read, who said: 'Maybe every novelist wants to write poetry first, finds he can't and then tries the short story, which is the most demanding form after poetry. And, failing at that, only then does he take up novel writing.'

Which has some truth in it, though about writers rather than about short stories. It is certainly true that far more people write short stories than read them, and true that most aspiring writers begin with the short story – they probably think that, because it is shorter than a novel, it must be easier, which is far from being the case. Faulkner is right there. I have always found writing a short story infinitely harder than writing a novel, if only because absolutely every word counts, there can be no slack and no hiding place. I also find that ideas come along with the form in which they need to be written, and those for the short story come along far less frequently than ideas for novels. I have no idea why. But a very few writers have committed themselves to the short story exclusively, or at least made their reputations by it, and have succeeded totally, magnificently, enviably.

There are a lot of short-story collections in this house and I could live for several months on them alone, though I wouldn't want to. I read a short story very occasionally, and carefully. Like poetry, they require a different sort of still, slow, intimate attention from the reader, and they also seem best when read one at a time. Follow one short story with two more and the impact of any one of them seems to be dissipated and diluted. I *re*-read short stories often. I have a handful of favourites that I know almost by heart. And if I have an idea for one myself, then I need to go back to these others and read them with great attention again, before I can start writing myself. It is not that I need to imitate, but I do need to be reminded and re-taught how it is best done.

It is a truism among publishers that there is no market for short stories. Magazines used to take them, from the weekly women's *Peg's Paper* which published Romances, through the middlebrow journals to those at the high literary end – the *Cornhill*, *Stand*, even the *TLS*. Nobody wants them now, except occasionally for a

Christmas issue. Anthologies pop up from time to time, published by writers' groups and small presses, heavily subsidised. Nobody buys them but people go on writing them, and reading them aloud in writers' groups, and submitting them to competitions, and there are correspondence courses which offer tuition in short-story writing and 'money back if not successful'. Perhaps, as with writing poetry, the activity is an end, and a satisfaction and fulfilment, in itself. It would need to be.

I have dumped an armful of short-story collections on the dining-room table. Goodness, I had no idea we were giving house room to so many. But in each volume, there is at least one which I read again and again, at least one which has helped me to learn how it should be done. Here are the Masters.

Guy de Maupassant, first read in French, for A level, but since then only in English. I suspect that the short story probably loses more than any other form (except poetry) in translation because of the intricacies of language and form. I remember feeling that, although I had read those set-text short stories of Maupassant almost off the page, yet I was still reading them through a fine mist, the veil that always stands between the reader and a language which is not his own.

The same must be true of Chekhov, and, as I know no Russian, he has only ever come to me in translation. But 'The Lady with the Little Dog' is on my list of essential short stories all the same. Better to read Chekhov in English than not read Chekhov at all. Is that true of any foreign writer?

Many novelists have also written short stories but very few bring off both forms with equal success. Novelist's stories sometimes wear a slight air of pointlessness, as if they were made out of leftovers – either that or the novelist has never quite found the short-story voice. And it is different. A short story is not just a short novel.

Here are two collections of short stories by P.G. Wodehouse, that comic genius. But they don't work, or not for me, because Wodehouse thrived on the leisurely approach, ambling up to a novel, taking the scenic route, and the short-story form does not work like that. Nor, I think, does it work for crime. The *Strand Magazine* used to publish short detective stories, and most nineteenth-century crime novelists turned their hand to the crime in short form, too. But crime also needs space in which to spread itself, to build, to engage with minutiae. So my perfect Collection contains no short crime, even by the best writers, even by Conan Doyle and Ian Rankin.

Alice Munro, Mavis Gallant, Grace Paley, Helen Simpson – my collections by these writers were huddled together. So far as I know, none of them has written a novel. They are all short-story writers first and last, though Paley also wrote poetry.

The trouble with Munro and Gallant is a sameness about all their stories. They blur together. I cannot distinguish between any of their characters because they are so alike, live the same ordinary lives in the same ordinary places. With Munro, the problem is Canada. I have a problem with Canadian as I do with Australian writers. (I know, I know.) But that is emphatically not true of America and strangely, though she too writes of ordinary people living ordinary lives, quite untrue of the stories of Grace Paley.

I interviewed Grace Paley at the Cheltenham Festival a few years ago. I greatly admired her work, and admired her record in campaigning for civil rights in her native America as much, so it was obviously an honour. It was also great fun. Grace was a wonderful talker and easy to interview because you just wound her up and set her going, and the audience was extremely appreciative. All went swimmingly, until the end, when I ushered Grace ahead of me down the short flight of steps from the stage, followed her, tripped and crashed headlong. The rest is something of a blur, but in the confusion of pain and attendants with walkie-talkies calling an ambulance and bringing blankets, I was aware of Grace bending over me with a look of tender concern and anxiety that I will never forget. Nor will I forget hearing what she said when, at that same moment, someone came up and asked her a question about her stories. She sounded quite shocked as she said, 'How can I talk about literatoor when my friend is so hurt?'

She called the hospital to enquire after me later that night and rang me when I got home, sent me flowers and a signed book with a card when she returned to America. I loved her. How could I not love her stories, or fail to include one in this imaginary perfect Collection?

Which seems to be coming along nicely, and may be useful to all those who want only the best on their shelves, a sort of crystallised or distilled library. My Collection will be all the short stories you will ever need – or I will ever need, for that matter. The toppling piles on the dining-room table can go.

Helen Simpson was one of those rare writers who mastered the short story completely from day one and the publication of her first collection, *Four Bare Legs in a Bed*. A friend said, 'We read Margaret Drabble to feel the zeitgeist, our daughters read Helen Simpson.'

She has an immaculate touch and seems to have been born with the ability to point up a story, pin down a situation, a place, a group of people, in the frighteningly small space that is the short story. I re-read a story of hers here, another there, and they come up in sharp, fresh focus every time. I have spent a while in choosing which one to put in my Collection and plumped for 'Burns's Night', from her last volume, because it captures the whole awfulness of a dinner full of braying, kilted, drunken, randy, rich, young bankers and business men, which in its turn captures a whole era that has evaporated into the mist.

Who else to select? William Trevor. John McGahern. Both Irish. Both very fine novelists. Both equally fine, and prolific, short-story writers, with that ultimate accolade, a book called *The Collected Short Stories of* ... They both go in, as they both go into any list I am required to supply, from time to time, of 'Writers Who Have Influenced Me' or 'My Ten Best'.

I am not going to let any of their work go, I need all of their stories, all their novels. I may have difficulty selecting one of each for my anthology.

No difficulty with Katherine Mansfield, surprisingly enough. I have found four separate selections from her short stories on my shelves, and three of them can go. The one to keep is essential as much for its long 'Introduction' by Elizabeth Bowen as for the stories themselves. Many an Introduction is a waste of space but Bowen never wasted a word and this is as good an essay on Mansfield as can be found: perceptive, thoughtful, densely argued, packed with insights – and utterly 'Bowen'.

I am picking two of Mansfield's stories. Not 'Bliss'. Not 'At the Bay', though many would argue for those. But I cannot be without one of the best stories ever written about childhood, 'A Doll's House', and her masterpiece, 'The Daughters of the Late Colonel'.

How often do I pick up a book by an author and move sideways to their biography? Always, with Katherine Mansfield, and the study of her by Claire Tomalin, best of biographers. The problem is that I cannot find it. I have a list here. 'Books I know I own but cannot lay my hands on'. It goes down on that.

V.S. Pritchett. D.H. Lawrence. Frank Sargeson. Frank O'Connor. Sylvia Townsend Warner. Raymond Carver. Henry James. All collected volumes of short stories but I have a gut feeling I won't read any of them again.

Ah, here is Muriel Spark, sharp as a pencil, cool, stylish, one of the rare writers whose stories are on a par with her novels for brilliance, another to put on the bedside table, another for the collection. 'The Black Madonna' should go in there I think, because it is quintessence of Spark.

In a small and separate pile are the ghost stories. It is the only literary genre I can think of which is overwhelmingly represented by the short story rather than the novel. M.R. James. Henry James. Dickens. L.P. Hartley. Edith Wharton, and many, many anthologies, for many a writer, past and recent, has written just one or two ghost stories. I wonder why. Did they have one 'true' story to tell? Were they specially commissioned for a handsome fee? Or did they just want to see if they could do it? My anthology will contain just two ghost stories – M.R. James's 'O Whistle and I'll come to you', and Edith Wharton's 'Mr Jones'. The other two I am going to re-read by the fire soon are novellas, so do not qualify – *A Christmas Carol* and *The Turn of the Screw*, and who will disagree that these are the two best ghost stories ever written?

I have found nine short-story anthologies of a mixed and general nature in the house and that is probably nine too many. Every compiler has their idiosyncrasies, every collection contains several stories whose inclusion I regard as totally unjustified, everybody chooses the wrong story by X or fails to put in one by Y. They just make me cross. I will do much better by myself.

Will I ever write another short story myself? I wish I knew.

# The Man with the
# Charming Smile

IT WAS PROBABLY 1962. Definitely London. Memory is like a long, dark street, illuminated at intervals in a light so bright that it shows up every detail. And then one plunges into the dark stretch again.

I have no idea in whose house the smart drinks party was held or out of whose kindness I was invited as a tyro novelist cum undergraduate. All of that has gone beyond recall, as have the faces of the other guests – though I remember waitresses in white aprons circulating with trays of cocktails.

The beam of light falls on a man standing leaning against a fireplace. His cocktail is on the shelf beside him. In his hand there is a cigarette holder. He has a high colour to his high cheekbones, a high forehead, too. High style. I am old enough to know that it is rude to stare but who would not stare at the craggy remains of such mesmerising good looks?

'Do you know Ian Fleming?' someone asks me.

I suppose that he said something to me, and there was a charming smile and crooked teeth and a waft of blue smoke from the long holder. It was over in a few moments because he was deep in conversation and laughter and I backed away, hoping to have become invisible.

So many people whose opinions I thought were important in those days sneered behind their hands at Ian Fleming and James Bond, though I daresay that, like Liberace, Fleming cried all the way to the bank. Why? Because the books were popular? Because they started being made into movies? 'Sex, violence and brand names,' one of my University tutors said about Bond with a dismissive wave of the hand. I often wonder if he had ever actually read any of them.

Here they all are, the Jonathan Cape hardbacks and the paperback versions, too, in their old stylish Penguin covers, not the hideous recent ones. Sometimes only a James Bond will do.

But, as people have come to understand, there is much more to Fleming than 'sex, violence and brand names', more than exotic travel, more than escapism – he writes so well, plots so well, does dialogue and structure and suspense and surprise so well. Some of the best stylists have been the greatest entertainers – Raymond Chandler. P.G. Wodehouse. And Fleming.

I could not get through my year without re-reading at least the best of the Bonds. *Dr No. From Russia with Love. Goldfinger. Casino Royale. You Only Live Twice*. How many thrillers can you re-read? They are disposable, open and shut, throwaway, leave-on-a-train books. To stand up to years of repeated readings there has to be more than blood and thunder, especially as, once you know what happens next, you lose the element of surprise.

But the villains, the settings and the set pieces, the friends back at the office – M, Miss Moneypenny – none of these fade over time, meeting them again is always a pleasure, just as escaping from sharks or roaring across a lake in a powerboat at full throttle or, perhaps best of all, sitting down at the casino table with James Bond, never loses its thrill.

Towards the end of Ian Fleming's life, when he was ill and out of sorts and temper, the only person whose company always delighted him was that of his close friend and editor at Jonathan Cape, the man he called 'gentle reader' – William Plomer. No one who knew William could be surprised at that. There was something enigmatic about both of them, a sense of hidden lives, other selves, an impression that behind the wholly civilised and gentlemanly facades something else was always going on.

The spy story holds a fascination all of its own. Fleming's, escapist, highly coloured, are a world away from those of the greatest spy writer of all, John le Carré, for he is deadly serious while Fleming is only semi-straight-faced – for much of the time he is joking. In a le Carré novel, the colour is drained away and, if Fleming writes well, le Carré is in a different league as a novelist. Every aspiring writer should be made to study his books to see how it should be done, how it is done best, but they would learn a thing or three from Ian Fleming as well.

Every so often, the dark stretches of memory give way to a moment or two when the light falls full on the handsome man with the high colour and the broken nose, leaning against the fireplace, glass to hand, smoke coiling from the cigarette holder. And the smile.

'Do you know Ian Fleming?'

# Children 3 Adults 0

IT IS HARD to remember that there was, and not so very long ago either, a world of children's books which did not contain Harry Potter, and the My Favourite Author lists were sometimes headed by Enid Blyton, sometimes by C.S. Lewis but most often by Roald Dahl. In the constant changing of the book-tide in this house, many volumes come and go but more children's books have earned a permanent place than any other genre, and Dahl is in no danger of losing his. His popularity was at its peak when my daughters were growing up. *Charlie and the Chocolate Factory*, *James and the Giant Peach*, *Charlie and the Great Glass Elevator*, *Fantastic Mr Fox*, *The Witches*, *Matilda*, *The BFG*, *The Twits*, *Esio Trot* … on and on they seemed to go.

One reason why some children's authors attain popularity among their young readers is, of course, because adults disapprove of them. It was one of the reasons we were all so devoted to Enid Blyton. Some parents are vociferously anti Jacqueline Wilson, who writes about dysfunctional families, step-children and teenage sex, and it has done J.K. Rowling no harm to have her books banned by fundamentalist Christian groups in America. Roald Dahl was disapproved of by adults because he believed that life was a permanent war between them and children, and he was always and everywhere on the side of the latter. Child anarchy is a dominant theme in his stories but children did not realise this consciously. They adored Dahl because he talked about snot and bums and made adults smell, but along the way, children recognised him as one of their own, and knew that he told riotously good, highly original, madly inventive stories in which magic invaded the ordinary world and extraordinary things happened casually, as they do in all the best fairy stories. That is what Dahl wrote, and he is in the greatest tradition. He is not afraid of frightening children, he knows they can take it, he is happy to point the finger at the duplicity and selfishness, and sometimes downright wickedness, of adults, going behind the masked smiles and cooing voices to reveal the real nastiness. Grown-ups can be cruel and stupid, snobbish and hurtful, and children know it. But meanwhile, there are the other worlds which Dahl so amazingly invented and which children flocked to enter. Some adults find his books disturbing because they know that each one conceals more than a grain of truth. Dahl liked to disturb and provoke. His short stories for adults pack a punch of absolute surprise, a single revelatory moment of horror. That is what the short story can do best. *Tales of the Unexpected* – the title is absolutely right.

I will re-read his children's books. I have not done so for twenty years. It will be interesting to see how they appear to me now that I do not have small children to defend against their terrors, even though they always alarmed me far more than they alarmed them.

Dahl's autobiographical books are here too, *Boy* and *Solo*, but an autobiography only reveals what its author intends, and they do not quite explain why Dahl was like he was – which, in my experience of him, was like a character out of one of his own books: slightly eccentric, contrary, enjoying being curmudgeonly, bad-tempered, autocratic – and burying any warmth, friendliness, affection, amiability, as deep as possible. But those qualities were there all right.

We met first in the 1970s when we were judging a *Daily Telegraph* short-story competition for which there had been, as there always are, many hundreds of entries. When we four judges met – the others were the literary editor of the paper, David Holloway, and the publisher Diana Athill, then senior editor with André Deutsch – we had undertaken to bring along a shortlist of just a dozen stories, having gone through the reading and weeding process for weeks beforehand. There was some overlap – three of us had several choices in common. Only Roald's list of stories was entirely different. Moreover, he ridiculed and derided ours, and would brook no arguments. He was having his way or he was walking out. Impasse. I have been on judging panels since where this has happened (though only one other where a walkout was on the cards). Only the tactful, patient persuasion of David Holloway kept Dahl in his seat and fended off more ructions. I do not remember the outcome but I know that we had to go away and re-read and change our minds and then return to be bullied some more before we reached a compromise – meaning, we decided to go along with what Roald wanted. He bullied us and I came away with a hearty dislike of the man. But I had not then read any of his children's books – and several of the best were still unwritten. Above all, I had not yet had children of my own. I did not get the point of Roald Dahl at all.

Fast-forward some fifteen years and I'm on another panel of judges with him, this time for the (now defunct) *Sunday Express* prize for fiction. The others were Clare Francis, Auberon Waugh and the literary editor of the paper, Graham Lord, and, once again, there were clashes. But Dahl seemed far mellower this time, and there were no threats of a walkout, or even much complaint, when his candidate did not win the £20,000 prize.

'He had a successful operation on his bad back and he's got a new wife,' Waugh whispered to me over the lunch.

On the off chance of his being in good temper, I had slipped my daughter's copy of *Charlie and the Chocolate Factory* into my bag and, as he seemed to be in an approachable mood, asked him if he would sign it. He did so cheerfully, then reached out for one of the notepads on the table and wrote 'Love to Jessica from Roald Dahl' on perhaps a dozen of the pages, tore them off and said, 'Give her these … she can sell them in the playground.'

After lunch we piled into taxis and went straight to the Café Royal and the prize-giving ceremony, but because of the traffic the cabs dropped us off on the opposite side of the road. Regent Street was, as ever, thick with cars and buses and the rest of us started to walk up to the nearest pedestrian crossing. Roald was having none of that. He was a tall imposing man and he simply raised his walking stick to hold up the traffic which was streaming towards us and stepped out into the road. It was like the parting of the Red Sea. We scurried over, all of us following him and his still-raised stick like embarrassed sheep, to the Café Royal, where a posse of professional autograph hunters lay in wait. Roald waved his stick at them. 'Go away. I only give autographs to children.'

A pain-free back and a happy marriage? Or just a lamb in wolf's clothing all along? I have the signed book here, together with a little pile of papers with his autograph – not sold in the playground after all.

Dahl was one of those geniuses who happen along only very rarely in the world of children's literature, someone who was totally in tune with the child's way of thinking, and view of life, and with exactly what children needed from their stories. His language, like his characters, like his plots, is sometimes anarchic, a firework display of inventiveness. He gave permission to children to be true to their real selves, not the selves grown-ups were trying to turn them into, let alone those their parents fondly imagine them to be. That is why children respond to his books and probably always will. His stories are timeless in their appeal because the quality of insight is recognised by each new generation.

Did he actually like children? He did more than that. He respected them for what they were, as relatively few adults ever do.

I revised my opinion of him totally, as who would not, but I daresay the grump was still in there somewhere ready to come out fighting.

# Decline and Rise?

IN THE SITTING ROOM are all the Iris Murdoch novels I have kept, all those I have guessed I may one day want to read again out of the twenty-six she wrote. I have kept the ones I love the best (rather than those I think the best) but who knows if those will be the ones that last? At present, her reputation is in the decline to near-oblivion that customarily follows the death of an author. It is the time – and it can last anything from five to fifty years – when novels sink and are forgotten as the reading world moves on, before someone plunges an arm into the depths and pulls up first one then another – and so begins the slow process of reassessment. In one sense, of course, Murdoch's novels will not have changed. How can they? And yet they have, because until it is read a book is a dead thing, it must be resurrected every time it finds a new reader, and those who read Iris Murdoch in the future will be very different people from the ones who read her now. They will have been formed in times unlike our own and will have different frames of literary reference. The novel and the way it is written will have changed, too. I first read Iris Murdoch's books as they were published. Novels were different then. People's tastes were different. The world around us was different.

Her books have not yet re-surfaced; they are not being assessed by new reading generations. Perhaps they never will be. Who knows that, either? There is no telling which writers will sink permanently, which will come up and be appreciated afresh, which ones may languish for seventy years or so before being found by some reader browsing among old books.

If I had to make a bet, it would be that *The Bell*, surely her best novel, will last, as will *The Sea, The Sea*, which won the Booker Prize. Perhaps the early ones – *The Sandcastle, Under the Net, Flight from the Enchanter* – will survive over the later. I have those, as I have *The Italian Girl*, because of its wonderful opening paragraph. But as time went on the novels became almost parodies of Iris Murdoch, and the last few seem clotted and overwrought.

But how could *The Bell* not be viewed as the classic that it surely is, ten, twenty, fifty years from now?

She is the mistress of the great set piece, the Dickensian or Hardyean scene in which characters and setting come together at some key moment in the plot, and heightened emotional tension is underlined by some momentous atmospherics – a weather event, perhaps, or some strange visual extravagance. In this novel the moment occurs when Dora and Toby secretly raise the great bell from the depths of the lake by pulling it behind the tractor, gazing at it as it emerges slowly, slowly and the water streams off its sides in the moonlight.

Critics stressed Iris Murdoch's metaphors, and the philosophy and ethical purpose binding her novels together, both underpinning and restraining the wilder flights of her imagination. Her humour tends to be forgotten but she was a comic writer with a rich sense of the risible in human portentousness and ambition. *The Bell* is about an informal Christian community based at a country house, Imber Court, situated in the grounds of a convent of enclosed nuns. Some of the mockery of the inhabitants' lack of self-awareness and spiritual pretensions is achingly funny. She looked at people with a clear, unprejudiced, unjaundiced but generally affectionate eye, a watcher on the periphery of the innumerable dances of friendship, love, courtship, marriage. She is especially good at families and their complex inter-relationships. The early novels are breathtakingly well plotted, so that we read on with a sense of real excitement. Will the pale and beautiful Catherine really take her solemn vows and enter the convent? Is her brother, the sinister Nick, with his shotgun and his dog, a force for evil? What desperate secret drives the man who heads the Imber community? All of her novels race ahead, with the reader clinging on madly through twists and turns and astonishing revelations, among huge casts of characters as varied and strange as those of Dickens.

Halfway through *The Bell* is a scene in which a group of madrigalists sing:

The silver swan that living had no note,
When death approached unlocked her silent throat.
Leaning her breast against the reedy shore
She sang her first and last, and sang no more.

I have only to read that to hear it, sung not by a choir but by Iris herself and her husband John Bayley on one foggy Sunday, after lunch at the house of a friend in Warwickshire. They had arrived in a battered grey pickup van, eaten, talked and drunk copiously, and then, with Iris sitting on a cushion beside the log fire and John in a low chair beside her, quite suddenly and without any apparent signal passing between them, let alone for any apparent reason, had begun to sing. They had light, wavering but not untuneful voices and everyone fell silent to listen. It could have been funny, a madrigal sung by these two small, oddly gnome-like figures, one of the country's leading novelists, and a distinguished don and man of letters. In fact, it was rather moving.

I interviewed Iris about her work on Radio 4 in the early 1980s. She was her own best critic, explaining, elucidating, but slightly distracted because she was due to meet her mother in a pub after the recording and was anxious not to be late in case harm befell her.

I did not see her often after that, but every meeting was memorable. My elder daughter shared a birthday with her and Iris once gave me a detailed briefing about their star sign – Cancer. I would see her walking slowly home down the Banbury Road laden with groceries in carrier bags and always refusing a lift. 'We should all walk more.' My children's school was in the next road to their house and she once stopped me to ask my four-year-old if she was learning to sing. 'You should sing,' she told her earnestly. 'It is so good for you.' I remembered 'The Silver Swan'. I am saddened that so many people only knew of her from the books and film about her decline into the darkness of Alzheimer's disease, which stripped her of her wit and humour, her gaiety and genius – but above all of her dignity.

The last time we met, she had indeed begun that decline, yet somehow her dignity was still intact. I was signing books at a charity sale in the Bishop's House in Oxford when the door opened on John, followed by Iris, dressed, by him no doubt, in a long, beige mac and a funny little tweed pork pie hat. It had been perhaps ten years since I had seen her. She was the same and yet dreadfully different, recognisable and yet a complete stranger. But I did not then know how far away from us she might actually be and I was so pleased to see her that I got up and took her hands and told her so. Her troubled, puzzled eyes looked into mine for a long time, searching anxiously for some clue, I suppose. John brought a cup of coffee and a biscuit, sat her down at my table and fed her, moistening small pieces of the biscuit and popping them into her willing mouth. And then, all of a sudden, a split second of awareness transformed her face, like the sun coming out from behind a cloud. Was it recognition? Probably not. But there was a connection between us, as she took hold of my hand and held it very tightly, and smiled. It didn't seem to matter whether she had any idea that we had known one another in another life or not. I wanted to thank her. I wanted to say something that would remind her of who she was and what she meant to so many of her devoted readers. But I could not think of the right words, just let her hold my hand for a few more moments, and watch the brightness fade gradually from her eyes, leaving nothing but vague panic.

And then John took her away.

I have lined up the novels of hers I have in order of publication. I should not have let any go, I realise, they are all of a piece, the good and less good, and all make up the strange genius of the novelist who was Iris Murdoch.

I have read books about her and somehow every one seems to describe a completely different woman – the fierce, passionate young Iris, the philosopher, the tutor, the lover, the famous novelist, Dame Iris, and I daresay they are all, in their way, true. She was not easily pinned down. I can only remember the Iris I knew, not closely, not well, but with honour and respect and with singular affection.

# Forgotten

JOHN BRAINE. ALAN SILLITOE. David Storey … names from the fifties. Storey *is* remembered as a fine playwright, but does anybody now read his novels, so influential to those of us growing up among books and writers of that decade and the one following? *This Sporting Life* and *Radcliffe* sit alongside John Braine's *Room at the Top* and Sillitoe's iconic *The Loneliness of the Long-Distance Runner* in old orange Penguin editions, their titles reminding me of the rise of the working-class novelist which changed the ways of publishing for ever. I re-read the Sillitoe a year or so ago and it stands up to the test of time pugnaciously, but sitting alongside it I have found another novel. I thought it a minor masterpiece when I first read it but that was thirty years ago. I have decided that reading from home must include books of which I once had a high opinion of some kind – that is, I once thought them very funny, wonderfully well written, original, or just very enjoyable. I have kept a number which seem to have earned their place, though time changes the books one loves.

Will I still rate John Wain's *The Smaller Sky* highly? I have put it on my bedside table. I am going to read it over the next few nights. Will I want to keep it on the shelf of assorted paperbacks next to the pinball machine?

Yes, is the answer to that, a week later. Yes, with some minor reservations. *The Smaller Sky* is not a perfect novel – but then, how many are? It seems dated, which is fine, but, in a way, not quite dated enough and that is true of a lot of novels of the 1950s and 1960s. I had forgotten how very moving it is. It is a poet's novel, not because it is written in lyrical language, certainly not because it is over-written which is what 'poetic' often means when applied to prose. But John Wain was a poet of some distinction, and that is evident in the way he shapes *The Smaller Sky*, in its beautifully bal-anced structure and its imagery, and the wonderfully evocative descriptions.

It seems at first to be a quiet and rather low-key book, yet it is really a passionate plea for individual freedom and a howl of rage at the conventions, restrictions and insensitivities of some human institutions. John Wain was not one of the Angry Young Men for nothing.

The hero, Arthur Geary, is a middle-aged commuter, conscien-tious and weary, dutifully supporting his wife and family, successful enough and apparently contented. And then he begins to hear drums beating frenziedly inside his head. His response is to run away, to escape into a life of perfect order and calm lived entirely on Paddington station, for here alone the drums in his head are silenced. Geary is law-abiding, he has saved money which he sends regularly to his family. He now wants to save his sanity. But shouldn't someone 'rescue' him? Surely he cannot go on as he is.

What about his family, his job, his nice home and his reputation?

Various people – friends, colleagues, experts – try to persuade him to return to the 'normal' world but none of them deflects him from his purpose. They are no more annoying than gnats buzzing round. But his relationship with his son David is a different matter. Wain has written an utterly convincing, honest and sensitive account of the deep, inarticulate, agonised love of a father for his brave, confused and lonely child.

> Something seemed to break inside Geary. It was as if, inside his chest, he had been carrying his feelings in carefully contrived glass containers. Now the containers shattered and his chest was flooded with blood, mush and broken glass. He opened his mouth to say something but the possibilities jammed his brain. He wanted to say that he would leave the station and come home with David then and there. He wanted to invite David to move into the hotel with him. He wanted to explain to David about the drums. He wanted to promise David that he would leave the station hotel within a week and find a place to live where David could come and stay every school holiday. Beyond all these things he wanted to say something that would lift the cold weight from David's heart and from his own. Nothing came and he allowed his mouth to close, drooping at the corners. Father and son looked at each other across the impersonal furniture.

John Wain wrote other novels – *Hurry on Down* is probably the best-known, but I wonder if this, or his poetry, or some very good short stories, have that extra touch of genius that makes *The Smaller Sky* a classic. Forgotten, probably. But still a classic.

# Writing in Books

THE ONLY SORT of writing in books I never do is of my name in
the front, though a few books which I owned as a child have my
full name inscribed, in ink, and some even have name, address
followed by *England, Great Britain, Europe, The Northern Hemi-
sphere, The World, The Universe, The Solar System, Outer Space* ...
do children still do that ? I hope so.

Some people continue to write their names in books all their
lives, others write in the books they give to others. As I often buy
books from second-hand shops, charity shops, bazaars, church
fetes and junk stalls, I seem to have acquired many cast-offs with
their provenance inked in. 'To Mr Battle, with best wishes from
Form V.'

'Aunt Em, Happy Birthday from Laura.'

'Mr John Gregory Mountford, from his mother.'

'To Annie from Frank. Christmas 1944.'

'Love to Dad from Ena, May, Jo, Phyl and Rodney, Hoping this
will give you something to laugh at.'

'To Squadron Leader Bendix on his Retirement.'

Who were they? Why did they give this book to that person? Did that person enjoy it? Why did they not keep it?

There was once a fashion for writing on the flyleaf: 'If this book should chance to roam/Smack its b.m and send it home.'

I stopped putting my name inside my books when I was fourteen and I never inscribe any I give as presents, though I sign plenty of copies of my own novels, as every writer does. It's a pretty debased currency, the author's signature. No wonder Roald Dahl only signed for children.

Happily, I can go among all our books without finding a single volume bearing a bookplate. Bookplates are for posers, even when beautifully designed by real artists and engravers, though most people claim they are only there to identify the owner in case of loss. I don't believe that. Do people put ID plates inside their hand-bags and wallets, or etch them on the family silver and china? Of course they don't, and only children have name-tags sewn into their clothes.

Yet the people who deface the front of a perfectly good book with their stuck-on bookplate are always the first to throw up their hands in horror when someone like me writes all over the text. 'Defacing a book' was one of the things you promised solemnly on the Bible never to do when you joined the library and that was fine, library books being borrowed, never owned.

But my books are mine to scribble in. When I first went to uni-versity, I had to own some textbooks because they were needed for a long, intensive period but the price of new textbooks being then, as now, prohibitive, I did what everyone did and bought second-hand from final-year students advertising them on the college noticeboards. By the time I had my Anglo-Saxon Primer, my *Beowulf* and *Ancrene Wisse* and *Sir Gawain*, Middle English verse and prose, and Robinson's edition of Chaucer, they had gone through many generations of King's undergraduates and the margins were thick with annotations, stanzas underlined and double-underlined. It was a badge of honour to own a book in which there were more pencilled annotations and comments and footnotes than lines of printed text, just as it was de rigueur to own a fifteenth-hand red and blue King's scarf. I wonder whoever bought a new one? Somebody must, but if so, they dropped it into the dust of the Strand and Surrey Street and trampled all over it many times before wearing it. I did not see a pristine, un-annotated textbook outside a library for my three years as a student, and the habit of making notes in the margin was formed for life. I scribble, underline, note, add, cross out, put in exclamation marks, turn down corners – even sometimes jot down phone numbers and PINs, and reminders to buy cat food. Not in every book – some pass through me undigested, bought, read, passed on. There is nothing in them worth noting or underlining.

Perhaps the idea that books are sacred and should never be marked or otherwise sullied goes back to the time when each one had to be hand-copied by a scribe; and then a little later, when they were expensively printed, also by hand and bound in that way, too, so that you would no more have scribbled in a book than you would have carved your name into the gateleg table in your morning room. When books were so rare and costly, people did not spend hours of their lives transcribing and printing rubbish, but once printing became a mass process and books cheap, the book, inevitably, was no longer sacred. If you discount fine, private press books, and expensive coffee-table volumes which are made to be looked at and admired but which only retain their value if they are in near-mint condition, books are not in themselves objects of worth. A paperback blockbuster may be left about, thrown away and scribbled in; and who is to say that my marginalia on the text of *Sir Gawain and the Green Knight* were not of great value to whichever student bought it from me when I left King's?

Antiquarian booksellers, whose trade is in books but who rarely seem to read them, like it if a book is an 'Association copy' – so my first editions of the James Bond books would be worth a lot more if they were all signed by Ian Fleming and inscribed to me, but a lot less if anything was written in them by another. Most of our first edition children's books have lost value in antiquarian eyes because they have names and addresses and even 'If this book should chance to roam …' inked inside and if I had known or cared about it, I would never have filled in the puzzles in my 1940s *Rupert Bear* annuals, or the crosswords in those very first issues of *Eagle* and *Girl*. But I did, and I am glad I did. That was what they were there for, just as the dot-to-dots were there to be joined up by my children, not for some future monetary gain.

I have a signed first edition of Virginia Woolf's *The Years*. I wish she had thought to scribble in it, too.

Not all the books in this house are defaced, and none bears a bookplate. But they are well worn and well read, well used and well loved and sometimes well annotated – and if there are any dot-to-dots, I will have joined them up.

# Who's Afraid?

THERE ARE SOME in every room, on every shelf and bedside table, though the two main collections are kept together, the best in the alcoves beside the drawing-room fireplace, the rest next to Thomas Hardy in the Small Dark Den. That is 113 assorted books by or about Virginia Woolf, and a few on Bloomsbury in general, with a run of the sadly short-lived *Charleston Magazine* thrown in. Easy to remember where it all began but harder to explain why a youthful interest which accorded with my aspirations at the time should not only never have faded but have greatly increased over so many years. Where are such passions formed, not only for an author and their work but for everything surrounding them, their lives, family, friends, the places in which they lived, their psyches? Not that I am alone in this particular literary obsession. The Virginia Woolf and Bloomsbury industries have gathered momentum and grown to vast and international proportions over the last fifty years. But when I first came upon her, she was far less known and it is hard to appreciate that then, in 1958, she had been dead only seventeen years and there was not very much literature about her. Her novels were read, though often dismissed by writers of the realistic twentieth-century novel – the successors to those formed in the very same realistic mould against which Woolf herself had reacted.

Writers learn to write most of all by studying books by other writers – the best, the great ones. One or two become all-important to us and formative, though why they should speak more than the others do, who knows?

I had never heard of Virginia Woolf when I was starting to write my own first book, aged sixteen, and chanced upon *A Writer's Diary* on the shelves of Coventry Public Library. I was hungry for anything that would not only teach me how to write novels but would tell me about how to *be* a writer, whatever I thought that meant, anything which would reveal the secrets of the writing life. It is hard to convey the excitement with which I read it.

*A Writer's Diary* has been close at hand, usually beside my bed, for the fifty years since then. I have a first edition, well thumbed and annotated, and a couple of paperbacks. I was enthralled by this extraordinary woman and her work and I have been so ever since. She was unique, a genius, a rare and strange artist as well as an ordinary, thinking, feeling human being, and of course her writing life was like no other – yet it can stand for so many others.

I learned how each novel germinated and grew, how she worked, sometimes quickly, before slow, painstaking revision and how she wove life around her writing and wove writing into her life, how she thought of it night and day, the constant background to everything else, how anxious she became about it, how ill it could make her – all of it was revelatory to me as a beginner. It still is.

The diary introduced me to the woman and led me to her books, and the shock of discovering her style, the passionate observations of life and places and people, has never really left me. I pick up *A Writer's Diary* every day, at random. It opens on her description of visiting Thomas Hardy, or on her ecstatic race across the final pages of *The Waves*, on the account of a lunch with Dame Ethel Smythe, on how hurt she is by a bad review in *The Times*, on Leonard's opinion of *To the Lighthouse*, or how she cares that Lytton Strachey is getting more attention than her. It has so many moods, contains so much intelligence, opinion, feeling – and gossip. It is a record of the times through which she was living while writing. The whole of Bloomsbury is here, in swift, intimate pen sketches which reveal the people to us as well as many a lengthy biography. I do not like most of them as I like Virginia but they are endlessly interesting.

I have never exhausted *A Writer's Diary*, and never will. It gave me what I needed at sixteen, and it continues to give. And it led me to the rest of the work – and that has to be its greatest gift of all.

I do not love all of her novels. I have never got on with *The Waves*, which always reminds me of the sort of highbrow radio play they used to broadcast on Radio 3, and the charm of *Orlando* passes me by. But I re-read *Jacob's Room*, *The Years*, and her masterpiece, *To the Lighthouse*, frequently and – test of great novels – find something new in them each time. As I grow and change, and my experience of life has increased, so those three novels appear slightly different, in the light of the time that has passed.

On the whole, I prefer to keep a writer out of their work. I do not feel that I myself or my life bear much relation to mine, nor would I ever expect someone who liked my books necessarily to like me. But with Virginia Woolf it is different. I am drawn to her, though I think it probable that we would have found nothing to say to one another.

I picture any encounter as rather like the one I had with Edith Sitwell. But Woolf was one of those fathoms-deep people. The more one reads her fiction and even more, her diaries, letters and essays, the more one discovers what made her tick, how she thought, what she stood for, why she wrote as she did, why her life was as it was. And, like ripples in a pond, interest in her does widen out to those around her, Leonard in particular, and also her sister, Vanessa Bell, and the Charleston set. The very male, ratiocinative, intellectual atmosphere of Bloomsbury, and especially of the Apostles, is not attractive. I have no biographies of Strachey, G.E. Moore, Keynes, et al. on my shelves but plenty of books about the Omega Workshops, Charleston, Vanessa Bell and Duncan Grant's paintings. I think Woolf is often misrepresented – so much is made of her frequent ill-health and fragile mental state and the agonies writing seemed to put her through that the more practical person is forgotten. But when she and Leonard started their own publishing firm, the Hogarth Press, they bought a printing press which she learned to operate; she fulfilled orders, packed the parcels and tied them with string, liaised with whoever they got in to help them in the office downstairs and with the person who went out to sell their books.

I knew one of those 'sales reps'. George (Dadie) Rylands was a young man when he went to work for the Woolfs and he left after a short time to take up a Fellowship at King's College Cambridge, where he remained for the rest of his long life. By the time I met him, at one of the Stratford-upon-Avon international Shakespeare conferences which he usually attended, he was in his seventies, cherubic of face, with soft, rather pink, skin and a fluff of white hair. There was something strangely child-like about Dadie, a sort of impish innocence.

He was a wonderful talker, full of jokes and giggles, and he would talk about Virginia if you wanted him to, though I daresay he got tired of all the Bloomsbury pilgrims to his rooms in King's. I used to look at him, as I also looked at William Plomer, another friend of the Woolfs, in bemusement that here they were, chatting to me, and there they had once been, chatting to Virginia. I suppose it is only the 'danced with a man who danced with a girl who'd danced with the Prince of Wales' syndrome, but it meant a lot. I have a snapshot of Dadie in Stratford with my daughters, taken so that they, too, would join in towards the end of that line of dancers.

When I sat my finals it was in the University of London Examination Halls in Gordon Square, the same Gordon Square in which Virginia had lived for so many years, round which she had walked so many times. It was good to remember that and feel the link, as I was answering the Modern Literature Paper question about her. I'm sure she helped.

But what if I had to choose only a dozen titles from my Woolf collection to last me for the rest of my life, whether that is a day, a week, or the thirty-three years needed to take me to my century? Almost everything must go. What am I to keep to see me through? Virtually every single book of academic literary criticism about Woolf would have to go. This is no time for critics. But a good biography is worthy of its place and I will keep two. Quentin Bell was Virginia's nephew, and so his biography is written from within her world. It is brief, it is affectionate but unprejudiced, and he wrote most beautifully. I have several other biographies here. Lyndall Gordon's is excellent, Hermione Lee's, too, but I think I will keep one which marries her life and her work, her mind and her writing and her emotions, by perhaps the best of the women who have written about Woolf: Julia Briggs's *Virginia Woolf: An Inner Life.* (American scholars have been to blame for most of the sillier flights of fancy and a fair old load of rubbish, too, about her state of mind and even her unconscious.)

John Lehmann was one of the young people who worked for the Woolfs in the basement room which was the nerve centre of the Hogarth Press, and his account of *Virginia Woolf and her World* is as good a short introduction to just that as you could find. His book was one of a valuable series published by Thames and Hudson and now all out of print, but I have a good selection of them. They have not been bettered as clear and straightforward accounts of writers in the context of their lives and times, and all with well-chosen illustrations.

Here is a book not about Vanessa Bell but by her, *Sketches in Pen and Ink: A Bloomsbury Notebook*, the nearest she came to writing an autobiography. It is a series of gracefully written pieces originally written for the informal Memoir Club which flourished among the Bloomsbury set from 1920. Vanessa Bell did not write very much, she communicated most of what she wanted to say via her paintings, but these short pen portraits are a delight and somehow distil the essence of the life lived by the Stephens sisters (as they were before marriage), their family and friends.

Only eight left? I will squeeze Leonard Woolf's own autobiography into a single huge volume, then, which leaves me seven of Virginia. *Jacob's Room*, *Mrs Dalloway*, *To the Lighthouse*, *The Years*, *A Writer's Diary*, one volume of the *Common Reader* and the *Selected Letters*. That's all? That's all.

But I have the essence of her here. If I re-read every one of the dozen over and over again I will still not have exhausted or fully understood the strange, mysterious, fascinating woman that is Virginia Woolf.

But what if I could have only one?

I can get it down to two, *Mrs Dalloway* and *To the Lighthouse*.

You choose for me, please.

# The Dregs?

WHAT IF I were left with only the books I call 'the dregs'. I have been rounding them up today. How did any of them get here? Who bought them, and when, and why on earth? Were they given to one of us or abandoned here by a visitor? Some are clearly witness to a passing phase in the life of a member of the family. Here is a book called *How to Train your Aggressive Dog*. But we have never had an aggressive dog. *Chinese Herbal Medicine for Everyday Ailments*? I flirted with homeopathy years ago, never with Chinese herbalism, but I am doubtless full of misinformation and prejudice about it so I suppose I should read it and learn. But then, what is an 'everyday ailment'? Who bought this stuff about how to get rich or to be a tycoon, or the autobiographies of those terrifyingly wealthy people in the *Dragons' Den*? Am I really going to be left only with books about how amateurs have taken over the internet or whether capitalism is dead? I know where the scattering of horse books came from, the guides to dressage and show-jumping and stable management, but now that we only have

Border Terriers I would not find *Breeding Golden Retrievers* of use. Imagine having nothing to read in the house but cookery books.

I have always been interested in the weather so books about clouds, the wrong sort of snow and a history of English weather do not count as dregs any more than do Anthony Holden and Amarillo Slim and Al Alvarez's brilliant books about poker. You do not have to play poker – though I once did – to find the psychology of those who spend their days and, even more, their nights at it interesting, or the history of the World Series in Las Vegas as glamorous as that of Hollywood. Those do not go into the box marked dregs, just on the shelf marked 'Random'.

Non-books do, though. Small hardbacked books bought in the run-up to Christmas or Valentine's or Mother's Day are non-books. They are about Everything Being Rubbish or how to microwave a budgerigar or where to go before you die, or why Slough is the armpit of the universe; they are little anthologies of love poems or things read at funerals or cartoons about politicians. Non-books breed, too. Books about Everything Being Rubbish breed others the same or, contrariwise, books about Everything Being Wonderful; old-fashioned recipes from Grandma's kitchen breed Grandpa's allotment tips. No one is expected to sit down and read a non-book from cover to cover but they come in handy for Boxing Day, when people lie idly in front of the fire flipping through them and laughing maddeningly and reading bits out to the assembly who read out bits from their own non-books in turn. After Christmas, their place is the charity shop but, as such books are often rather small in stature, they manage to hide themselves in the cracks between normal books and so go unnoticed, sometimes for years. Often, when they come to light again, so much time has passed that they've been transformed into items of nostalgia, like old annuals, and can be brought out and read aloud in a different tone of voice altogether. They remind us of the first Christmas with our in-laws, or the one when the cat shinned up the festive tree and brought it crashing down, Christmases in the 1970s. I have a book that reminds me of the time I was staying with friends for Christmas and had flu. Someone brought me a tray on which was a teeny tiny Christmas dinner, with a minute portion of everything, including a teaspoon of the pudding in which someone had carefully concealed one charm, and a thimbleful of wine. That Christmas was many years ago and the friend gave me a copy of Shakespeare's sonnets, bound in leather and no bigger than two postage stamps. Was that a non-book? I don't know, but I wish I could find it again.

Yesterday I went to a drawer I open only a couple of times a year because it contains nothing but a pile of hooks for suspending Christmas tree baubles, the spare bagatelle balls, and a box of matches, which was what I came in search of. But behind the matches were three very small books. One was an illustrated manual of knots, the second a collection of jokes made by President Ronald Reagan, and the third was called *Inspirational and Uplifting Quotations from the Scriptures*. I have absolutely no recollection of having seen any of these books before, nor a clue who bought or brought them, let alone why, though the knots might come in handy. Books about things like knots are all the rage again, now that there is a vogue for the 1940s and 1950s and facsimiles of manuals for Boy Scout signallers, and the like. Supposing one were stuck here for a year with only these three for intellectual stimulation and mental nourishment?

Or with:

*The Schoolgirls Pocket Book 1956* (though this does contain useful
  things to learn by heart)
*Red Grouse and Moorland Management*
*How to Construct a Questionnaire*
*Ecce Romani Book 2: Rome at Last* (I could brush up on my Latin)
*Psychology and Policing*
*Handbook of Festivals for the Jewish Family*
*The Cult of the Virgin Mary*
*Sue Barton. District Nurse*
*Ein hoff chwaraeon* (A Ladybird Book. I could learn Welsh)
*A Simple Guide to Filling in Your Tax Return* (1987)

Whatever kind of person would emerge after a year with only the
above for company?

# Not Met

THE OLDIE MAGAZINE has for years had a column called 'I Once Met'. I wonder how famous one has to be to appear in it as a 'not met.' I got into an index under that guise. To my amazement, when I first flipped through the index to Anthony Powell's autobiography before reading it, I came upon my own name. Hill, Susan. Novelist. (Not Met.)

Here is the long shelf in the sitting room devoted to the books of another heroine, Elizabeth Bowen. (Not Met.)

Bowen is a novelist who has come into her own in the last ten years, having gone into and emerged triumphantly from the limbo that awaits all writers when they die. Indeed, she had been falling into that limbo during the last years of her writing life, which was a disgrace; a greater disgrace is that, although her critical reputation has never been higher and there are some good new commentaries on her work, the novels sell relatively few copies and many are now out of print. Bowen is not known as well as she should be. I wonder why.

It may be to do with the clotted and slightly artificial style in which she sometimes wrote. Her novels are not like blancmange, they do not slip down easily; but the reward for tackling the prickly thicket of her prose is very rich and she is not very hard, not obscure, not irritatingly convoluted. If you can read Henry James, Bowen is a walk in the park.

I have biographies of her by Patricia Craig, Victoria Glendinning and Hermione Lee, as well as the more recent academic studies, and I could not part with any of them as each has its own view which complements and balances the others. Glendinning's is perhaps the best 'Life', though there might now be room for a new one because Bowen was one of those novelists whose life and times, the people and the places she knew well, really are relevant to her fiction, really do illuminate one's understanding of it. She was Anglo-Irish and that informs much of her work. I have two favourite novels and one is *The Last September*, about a great family and its house in the Irish countryside in 1918, at the height of the Irish War of Independence, and the novel brings those events, those times and places, more vividly home than any number of histories. But it is not a history, it is fiction, facts have been transmuted into art. It has an atmosphere about it which wraps the reader round. The family, their visitors, the older generations and the younger, are central to the novel, but perhaps the house itself is even more so. Places and their significance were extremely important to Bowen, in the way that they were to Hardy. Landscapes are much more than simply backdrops to events, houses have character in the way that human beings do – families fall apart in many of them, and, as Hermione Lee puts it, 'landscapes of dereliction are made to illustrate states of mind'.

I think that is why Bowen was so good at writing ghost stories. Ireland in particular is full of ghosts and haunted houses, and she understood that atmosphere and a sense of place are all-important to the success of the genre. Just as important as Ireland are London, and War (she once said that she did not quite know how she would manage without one). If you want to know what London was like during and in the aftermath of the Blitz, a bombed-out terrain of half-houses hanging almost in mid-air, of blacked-out streets, of rubble and waste ground across which valerian and ragged robin grew, read Bowen. If you want to know how people talked and walked and tried to go about their everyday lives and above all how there was a strange hollow at the heart of things, read Bowen.

The broad canvas is not for her. She expresses, describes, high-lights by a perfect use of detail – a lace doily with a few crumbs left on a plate, a pair of chamois-leather gloves being buttoned at the wrist, a man striking a match in the street to light the cigarette of a stranger, furniture, food, drink, items of clothing. She knows that detail can either be pointless, tiresome padding which contracts the reader's own imagination, or that it can be made to count, in the way it can somehow echo a sentence, illuminate a moment of choice, stand for a very particular emotional situation.

Bowen makes the reader think. You do not take sides with her characters, because, on the whole, she does not, but you come to understand them, to know what makes them tick and why they have become what they are.

Her stories can induce fear, the chill down the spine, a moment of horrified realisation at what is about to happen. They do not spread happiness – they are too clear-eyed for that. On the whole, they do not make the reader cry either, but there is one that I can never read without a pricking behind the eyes. *The House in Paris* is her master-piece. The structure at first seems disjointed but read it again and the central section, which explains those that bookend it, as the past explains the present, does, after all, fit exactly where it should.

The book is about two children, Henrietta and Leopold, who first meet at a house in Paris. Henrietta is travelling with a woman who is being paid to take her to her family in the South of France, and Leopold is about to meet his mother for the first time since infancy. Henrietta is a neat, precise, well-mannered, reserved little girl; Leopold is a rougher, more awkward boy, full of confused emotions, wants and dreads. In the dark, old-fashioned house, they are left alone together for hours and must somehow come to an understanding and an accommodation, if not a friendship. It is almost impossible. They are worlds apart and each for different reasons resists any identification with the plight of the other. Both are lonely, unhappy, strange little children, both have reasons for keeping themselves apart from one another, and the house.

It is a tense book. We read it with in-drawn breath. Bowen was one of the best writers about children, seeing them on their own terms as well as from the viewpoint of the adult outsider. She understood how cruel they could be to one another, how the small savage was so very close to the surface of the charming young person. I do not think that I know a fictional scene more poignant and moving than that in which Leopold finds out, finally, that his mother is not coming after all, and he starts to cry, his head against the mantel-piece in the cold formal room, Henrietta beside him, clutching her toy monkey, reaching out to touch him for the first time with a sort of unpractised and stiff comfort. All the dashed hopes and bitter loneliness, all the feelings of being rejected and unloved and entirely isolated from the rest of the world, come together, crystallised in this one scene which I can hardly bear to re-read.

All writers are asked about their influences and it is a hard question to answer correctly because almost everything we read is an influence, and usually quite unconsciously. Other people's ways of writing can surface in one's own years later, influences but barely recognisable as such. But a few are known and those few are the ones that strike a chord at the moment of reading. This is how it is done, this is how I want to do it. Elizabeth Bowen is one such for me. From the beginning, how she does what she does, the sort of people and places that are unmistakeably hers, were absorbed as I read, and read again. Writers are formed by their childhoods, by places which have given up their inner meaning, by people glimpsed, and above all by emotions both felt and observed. But they are also formed by other writers, other books, and I am very conscious that Bowen was one of those who formed me.

She knew a great many people of note, from her early years in Ireland, through to her marriage and time spent in Oxford and London. She had an interesting war. She was a handsome woman, with dramatic and arresting rather than beautiful features and she had a number of serious lovers of both sexes – but a rather lonely old age, as is so often the case among those who have outlived so many friends and had no family of their own. Through William Plomer I came to know her a little at the end of her life, via letters. We had planned to meet but cancer intervened and we never did. But I cherish her letters, written in a wild hand with lots of capital letters and loops. She was one of those people who gave herself to the page so that her personality came vividly across, and so I felt that I did know her, that we had met. It happens.

# Sebald

BOOK COLLECTIONS GROW organically and in part they grow according to mood so that one ends up with a library that runs the gamut, from frivolous to suicidal, and in this year I may be inclined towards both, and all shades of mood in between.

W.G. Sebald was German-born and lived and worked in England, as an academic – in his last years as Professor of Modern German Literature at the University of East Anglia. He wrote in German but the translations of his books seem so perfect, flexible and subtle in their choice of English vocabulary and syntax that if one had not been told that the books were translated, one would never have guessed. I know of no other writer like Sebald. Nobody does. He is totally European, and yet with a profound, if detached, understanding of England. His subject matter is extraordinary, unpredictable and odd – he seems to collect the unusual and be interested in the outlandish, but, through his eyes, even the ordinary and prosaic becomes somehow strange. Everything he sees, everywhere he goes, every person he meets, all are filtered through some curious lens of his own devising. He brings to a walk through a landscape, or an object or a memory or a historical anecdote, the entire weight and depth of his own vast reading and learning and knowledge. It is all lit in a unique, Sebaldian light.

But he is a writer who induces the most profound sense of melancholy. Over all his writing is a sort of miasma of existential despair. Is it that he chooses to visit places which are in deep shadow, hold memories of a terrible past, are bleak and run-down, poor and seedy and out of date, or is it that this is his permanent mood, a mood that somehow infects and alters places?

Sebald was a great walker (this accounts for the detail) and in *Vertigo*, he visits a village in the Tyrol he calls W, a place he has not seen since he was a boy. Having taken a bus from Innsbruck, he alights at the Oberjoch customs post, and starts to walk.

The gorge was sunk in a darkness I would not have thought possible in the middle of the day. Only, to my left, above the brook invisible from the path, there hung a little meagre light. Spruce trees, a good seventy to eighty years old, stood on the slopes. Even on those growing up from the depths of the ravine the evergreen tops did not appear until far above the level of the path. Time and again, whenever there was a movement in the air above, the drops of water caught in the countless pine needles came raining down. In places where the spruce stood further apart grew isolated beech trees that had long since shed their leaves, their branches and trunks blackened by the persistent wet. It was quite still in the gorge save for the sound of water at the bottom, no birdsong, nothing. Increasingly a sense of trepidation oppressed me and it seemed as if the further down I walked the colder and gloomier it became. At one of the few more open places, where a vantage-point afforded a view both down onto a waterfall and deep rockpool and upwards into the sky, without my being able to say which was the more eerie, I saw through the apparent infinite loftiness of the trees, flurries of snow high up in the leaden greyness ...

Not far from the margin of the forest stands the Krummenbach chapel, so small that it can surely not have been possible for more than a dozen to attend a service or worship there at the same time. In that walled cell I sat for a while ... What I remember most ... is the Stations of the Cross, painted by some unskilled hand round the mid-eighteenth century and half already covered and eaten by mould. Even on the somewhat better preserved scenes little could be made out with any degree of certainty – faces distorted in pain and anger, dislocated limbs, an arm raised to strike. The garments, painted in dark colours, had merged beyond recognition with the background, which was equally unrecognisable. Insofar as anything was visible at all, it was like looking at some ghostly battle of faces and hands suspended in the gloom of decay.

That walk through the dripping dark valley between the pines, and the scene in the tiny, cold chapel with its mouldy frescoes, could have been conjured up by almost no one but Sebald and, like so many others in his extraordinary books, cling to the walls of the memory like the atmosphere of a nightmare. The same seems to happen to him.

A good thirty years had gone by since I had last been in W. In the course of that time many of the localities I associated with it such as ... the parish woods, the tree-lined lane that led to Haslach, the

> pumping station, Petersthal cemetery where the plague dead lay, or
> the house in the Schray where Dopfer the hunchback lived, had
> continually returned in my dreams ...

The hotel, when he reaches it, is empty, hollow-sounding and
ghostly as any in a horror film.

> Behind the reception-desk ... after I had rung the bell several times
> to no avail, a tight-lipped woman eventually materialised. I had not
> heard a door open anywhere, not seen her come in, and yet there
> she suddenly was. She scrutinised me with open disapproval.

But so many places on a Sebald journey are eerie, deserted, out
of date, and lie under a pall of dismal weather. In *The Rings of
Saturn* he walks through East Anglia and manages to make places
I know well, and have found sparkling and lively, suicidally
depressing. Lowestoft is not one of the country's most prepossess-
ing of towns and has suffered like many others from neglect and
poverty but I do not remember its being as drear as Sebald finds
it.

> I walked for a good hour long the country road from Somerlayton
> to Lowestoft, passing Blundeston prison, which rises out of the
> flatland like a fortified town and keeps within its walls twelve-
> hundred inmates at any one time. It was already after six in the
> evening when I reached the outskirts of Lowestoft. Not a living soul
> was about in the long streets I went through, and the closer I came
> to the town centre the more of what I saw disheartened me ...

And as he leaves the town the next day, inevitably he passes a hearse.

> In it sat two earnest-faced undertaker's men … And behind them, in the loading area, as it were, someone who had but recently departed this life was lying in his coffin in his Sunday best, his head on a little pillow, his eyelids closed, hands clasped, and the tips of his shoes pointing up.

As well as being full of places which, if not already weird, become so through the Sebald lens, his books teem with curious people. He neither meets nor knows anyone unnoticeable, dull, ordinary, everyday and, also in *The Rings of Saturn*, he tells a story of an idiosyncratic man and woman which is so poignant that it turns into a sort of operatic tragedy which haunts the mind.

The book opens with Sebald in a Norwich hospital, after having had some form of nervous breakdown, looking out onto the city under a pall of grey cloud, from his room on the eighth floor. And he remembers Michael, a colleague at the University, typical of certain academics, wholly absorbed in their work, usually in some minor byway of an abstruse subject – careless of their appearance, detached from the rest of the human race and still children in most respects other than the mere physical.

> Michael was in his late forties, a bachelor and, I believe, one of the most innocent people I have ever met. Nothing was ever further from his thoughts than self-interest; nothing troubled him quite so much as the dire responsibility of performing his duties under increasingly adverse conditions. Above all, he was remarkable for

the modesty of his needs, which some considered bordered on eccentricity ... Year in, year out, as long as I knew him, he wore either a navy blue or a rust-coloured jacket, and if the cuffs were frayed or the elbows threadbare he would sew on leather trims or patches. He even turned the collars of his shirts himself ... It often seemed to me ... that, in his own way, he had found happiness, in a modest form that is scarcely conceivable nowadays.

Also then teaching at the University was Janine, a similar character, totally immersed in her work and her passion for Flaubertian minutiae. Sebald brings her to life and vividly re-creates her office:

where there were such quantities of lecture notes, letters and other documents lying around that it was like standing amidst a flood of paper. On the desk, which was both the origin and focal point of this amazing profusion of paper, a virtual paper landscape had come into being in the course of time, with mountains and valleys. Like a glacier when it reaches the sea, it had broken off at the edges and established new deposits all around the floor, which in turn were advancing imperceptibly towards the centre of the room. Years ago, Janine had been obliged by the ever-increasing masses of paper on her desk to bring further tables into use, and these tables, where similar processes of accretion had subsequently taken place, represented later epochs, so to speak, in the evolution of Janine's paper universe. The carpet, too, had long since vanished beneath several inches of paper; indeed, the paper had begun climbing from the floor, on which, year after year, it had settled, and was now up the walls as high as the top of the door frame, page upon page of memoranda and notes pinned up in multiple layers, all of them by just one corner.

Neither of these two academics could survive in any university today – indeed, it is a wonder they survived then, but somehow their childlike eccentricities, a retreat from the real world in which people must grow up, were tolerated and they managed to carve out harmless corners in which they could live and defend themselves against the encroachments of responsible adult life.

Of course, the story is a tragedy. Michael died one night, alone in his Norwich house, presumably of natural causes and the shock affected Janine more deeply than anyone.

> One might say that she was so unable to bear the loss of the ingenuous, almost childlike friendship they had shared, that a few weeks after his death she succumbed to a disease that swiftly consumed her body.

She had clearly been profoundly in love with a man who would never have known it – for she would never have been able to express it.

Time is the connecting thread running through Sebald's books, time and a sense of place. The past and how it lives on inside oneself, the decay of the solid edifices of the past and how their fragmentary remains are found in the present, are constant themes.

He is a writer for whom melancholia is a semi-permanent condition and who could probably never have produced a book had it been otherwise.

The story of Michael and Janine reminds me of a novel which has become woven into the fabric of my reading life. Love is the most difficult thing to write about successfully. It is the litmus test of greatness in a novelist if a love story moves and convinces and never once makes the reader grimace, smirk or feel embarrassed. Modern novelists are bad at writing about love because they feel that it has to mean writing explicitly about sex. On the whole, it was Dickens's one great failing, too, because it brought out the sentimental in him, whereas Thomas Hardy succeeds every time. Graham Greene is one of the moderns who best conveys a great many aspects of love, whereas D.H. Lawrence is mawkish. Virginia Woolf did not often try, probably because other human relationships interested her more. The classic French novelists did it well. The great Russians are pre-eminent.

But I know one novel which tells more than any other about unrequited love, foolish love, and love which matures, after a poor start, into greatness; a novel that pierces to the heart of the sort of love that endures to death and beyond, without ever having been fulfilled. It is a small, quiet novel by a writer who was first published at Leonard and Virginia Woolf's Hogarth Press and was admired both by them and many of their circle, including E.M. Forster and Lytton Strachey.

My copy of *The Rector's Daughter* by F.M. Mayor is quite battered but I have never bought another because I am so fond of it. It has been on long train journeys with me, I have read it during delays in airports and in a tedious hospital bed. And it has never failed me – never failed to make me forget myself and everything going on around me, never failed to move me beyond tears.

It reminds me a little of Sebald, though I read it long before I had heard of him, because it is set mainly in a small village in East Anglia, the sort of uninteresting, unprepossessing village which has neither beauty, character nor charm and which would probably have held great appeal to him for those very reasons.

Dedmayne is a place he might have walked through on one of his long tramps.

> There was no great house with park or garden to give character to the village. Progress had laid hold of it fifty years before and pulled down and rebuilt the church, the rectory and most of the cottages. Part of Dedmayne was even ugly; there was a bit of straight flat road near the church, with low dusty hedges, treeless turnip fields, and corrugated iron roofs of barns which might rank with Canada. Dedmayne was on the road to nowhere … the grimy Blue Boar did not induce anyone to stop for tea. Still, being damp it was bound to have certain charms.

In the rectory lives Canon Jocelyn, parson and classical scholar, an old-fashioned, reserved but not cold man whose beloved wife died many years before and whose sons have both long left home and never returned. He has one mentally handicapped daughter who dies early in the novel, and Mary. It is Mary on whom the novel focuses, and Mary's circumscribed spinster life, good works in the parish, secret poetry-writing, occasional moments of furious frustration and passionate desire to escape, soon quashed. Into Dedmayne, and this bleak but calm and not unhappy life, comes the Reverend Herbert, son of an old friend of Canon Jocelyn and newly appointed to a nearby parish. Mary and Robert Herbert become friends, then close friends, with so much to say to one another, so much in common, so many lonely years to make up for. Of course, Mary falls in love, a love so profound it is almost frightening, and also so open and vulnerable, so hopeful and innocent, and all the more so for being a first love come late. Robert Herbert loves Mary, too, cautiously and silently though he is never, at least at this point, as deeply in love as she is, but they are perfectly suited and seem destined for marriage. And then the blow falls.

The author of *The Rector's Daughter*, Flora Mayor, was an unusual woman, the daughter of a clergyman who held the chairs first of classics, then of moral philosophy, at King's College, London. Before turning her full attention to writing she spent some unlikely years pursuing a career on the stage. She did not live in a bleak vicarage in flat East Anglia but in a cheerful suburban household in Surrey. But the novel is at least emotionally autobiographical. Flora Mayor became engaged to a young architect, who travelled to India to take up a post – she was to join him – and died there of typhoid and her hopes for marriage, children and a happy future were at an end. Unfulfilled, if not unrequited, love was something about which Flora Mayor knew much. I feel a closeness to her whenever I come upon her book. Flora Mayor's niece, Tess, was a friend, and one of the oldest friends of Dadie Rylands. She was also mother of Victoria Rothschild, who married Simon Gray, whose diaries have brought so much delight.

Sebald. East Anglia. F.M. Mayor. Tess. Victoria. Simon. My own chain of lighted rooms, I suppose.

One thing leading to another takes me down a different route to East Anglia and three shelves of books always kept together.

But I am not quite ready yet to open the door that leads to Benjamin Britten.

# Collection, Compilation, Miscellany, Omnibus, Anthology

IN THE UGLY oak bookcase at home was a book bound in maroon called *The Anthology of World Literature*, well over 1500 pages of the semi-transparent India paper you mainly find now in bibles and prayer books.

It opened, so far as I remember, with a selection of poems and wise sayings from the Ancient Chinese and then from the literature of Persia and Arabia. How romantic those names were. They still are. Persia. Arabia. Transylvania.

I inherited the anthology but I have failed to find it now. It will come to light, propping up some wonky chair. It's that sort of book.

I loved it as a child for the very reason that one does come to love anthologies – they are puddings full of plums. You open at random, dip, read, open again, dip, read, open … You can spend twenty minutes and find nothing of interest and the next day open it and fall upon something that leads into new worlds or which stays in your mind for the rest of your life.

I can never decide if anthologies are best compiled haphazardly or given a structure. *The Rattle Bag*, intended for school children but enjoyable at any age, is deliberately haphazard and its editors, Ted Hughes and Seamus Heaney, make a good case for that in their introduction.

That is the poetry collection I would rescue if the house were on fire, but there is a lot to be said for an anthology whose contents are like beads on a chain, placed with care, the chain itself forming the common thread.

*The Anthology of World Literature* did not tell me anything about the mind of the compiler, but that particular dimension is one of the most valuable things about some of the best anthologies. I wish I had been taught by David Cecil. A friend of mine was, and said that, although he enjoyed his tutorials at the time, he did not realise quite what a remarkable experience they had been until much later in life: memorable, enriching, eccentric but never wayward. Contact with a mind as well-stocked as that, and an academic and critical skill so refined, is worth everything. It is also one of the greatest benefits of the Oxbridge one-to-one tutorial system. At King's, we had tutorials for two, and as people were sometimes ill the two could easily become one, which could be alarming. Oxbridge, however, has always had one-to-one tutorials. Long may they continue (though the present-day financial situation of universities will probably ensure that they do not). Nothing helps focus the attention and train the critical faculties of an undergraduate, perhaps even a first-year aged eighteen and scarcely out of school, better than spending an hour discussing their subject with one of its world experts. And that was the way of it: professors did tutor students in their first term. Having David Cecil's *Library Looking Glass: A Personal Anthology* to hand is the next best thing to being his student. He shaped it (loosely) by following the alphabet, but you scarcely notice that and do not really need to. It is not only an extraordinarily wide-ranging, surprising, varied and thought-provoking selection of extracts from prose and verse, it has David Cecil's comments, observations, explanations, insights, too. Wherever you land in *Library Looking Glass* you learn something or take away an idea or a nugget of understanding. I have opened it at random on four lines from Herrick's poem 'To the Water Nymphs, Drinking at the Fountain'.

> Reach, with your whiter hands, to me
> Some crystal of the spring;
> And I about the cup shall see
> Fresh lilies flourishing.

That is charming, but I don't think it would strike me as much more without Cecil's comment:

> If Herrick had said 'white' instead of 'whiter' the charm of the first line would be lost. It is the use – now an obsolete use – of the comparative which makes this charm so compelling. It is an ambiguous charm; for, I suppose, that Herrick simply meant that the hands of the water nymphs were whiter than lilies. But the fact that this is only stated implicitly and elliptically suggests that they possess some

supreme ultimate radiancy of whiteness, that they are whiter than anything else in the whole world.

Time and again Cecil illuminates a passage in this way, or makes a pertinent suggestion as to an additional meaning.

Whenever I need to remind myself of the aim, object and function of literary criticism, I come to his crystal-clear, succinct summary. Has it ever been bettered?

> … [the literary critic's] aim should be to interpret the work they are writing about and to help readers to appreciate it, by defining and analysing those qualities that make it precious and by indicating the angle of vision from which its beauties are visible.
>
> But many critics do not realise their function. They aim not to appreciate but to judge; they seek first to draw up laws about literature and then to bully readers into accepting these laws … [but] you cannot force a taste on someone else, you cannot argue people into enjoyment.

I keep meaning to get that by heart but at least I have the page in which it appears (under C for Criticism) firmly turned-down.

Lord David's insights are not only literary. He quotes from George Savile, the Marquess of Halifax, the somewhat sobering line, 'Men must be saved in this world by their want of faith.'

His expansion of this seems very pertinent in years when fundamentalism and the extremes of belief are still in alliance with the forces of darkness and wreaking havoc around the world.

A profound truth though seldom recognised. It is often said that mankind needs a faith if the world is to be improved. In fact, unless the faith is vigilantly and regularly checked by a sense of man's fallibility, it is likely to make the world worse. From Torquemada to Robespierre and Hitler the men who have made mankind suffer the most have been inspired to do so by a strong faith; so strong that it led them to think their crimes were acts of virtue necessary to help them achieve their aim, which was to build some sort of an ideal kingdom on earth.

But as we have been told on very good authority, the Kingdom of Heaven is not of this world. Those who think they can establish it here are more likely to create a hell on earth.

Some of the alphabetical entries are predictable – Beginnings, Beauty, Humour, Food and Drink – but others are more unusual and give rise to more recondite and provocative entries. I like, under R, The Right Place for Reading, which begins with Lytton Strachey, who says 'Pope is doubtless at his best in the middle of a formal garden, Herrick in an orchard and Shelley in a boat at sea. Sir Thomas Browne demands, perhaps, a more exotic atmosphere.'

A typical Strachey passage and David Cecil remarks wryly that it is 'not very practical'. But he agrees that the 'art of reading does include choosing the right place to read in'. He then describes how he read Turgenev's *House of Gentlefolk*: 'in the front hall of a Munich hotel with people coming and going all round me and the place full of the noise of doors swinging open and shut and visitors giving orders about their luggage'. My eyes opened wider as I read this. I wonder if the Munich hotel was the Four Seasons. If so, I identify with him entirely, as I sat in the foyer there for an hour waiting for a taxi to the airport reading George Eliot's *Daniel Deronda*, a novel which was my good companion on a dull European book tour and staved off the tedium of many a hotel foyer and departure lounge.

I once had to spend an entire day, from just after seven in the morning until nine at night, on Milan station waiting for a night sleeper, and Graham Greene's *The Quiet American* and *The End of the Affair* are forever associated with that strange, lonely day among the marbled magnificence, echoing waiting rooms, and noisy arrivals and departures. For David Cecil, the foyer of the Munich hotel had such an impact because he had never been abroad before and, he remembers, 'my new and foreign situation made my imagination receptive to what was to me a new and foreign book'. He adds that 'It is a pleasure to read *The Aspern Papers* anywhere. It is an especial pleasure to read it in Venice, its home town.'

Indeed. The books may gain an extra dimension, one may understand something more. But for the most part, does it really matter what book is read where? I have read, or do read, on trains and boats and planes, in bed, on a sofa, in a window seat or a deckchair in the garden, in hotel lounges, on benches, even in queues. Not in cars. But I am puzzled by Strachey's linking authors to special places in which they are best read. Every linguistic nuance of a complex late Henry James novel might not be fully grasped standing on a crowded commuter train or in a room of noisy schoolchildren – on the other hand, concentration might effectively blot out the outside world and be every bit as intense as in a silent library. I have seen people on the underground reading extremely difficult books as well as the sort that glide over you, leaving no trace. Perhaps a ghost story is enhanced by fireside reading at night with the wind rattling the casement. Perhaps *Wuthering Heights* might do well under those circumstances, but it doesn't follow that other, very different, books would not work there.

Is it better to read books about England when abroad, or accounts of travel to far-flung exotic places when safely in a suburban living room? Won't either do? I think this is a false trail. But if so, it's one of the very few in David Cecil's satisfying anthology. It is quite idiosyncratic and reveals not only Cecil himself, teacher, reader, scholar, but is a mirror of his times, although it was published only in 1975, for it is full of authors known intimately to him and his generation of well-educated, civilised men. Of course, he knew well, and quotes in it, many authors who are still read and studied today: Shakespeare and Wordsworth, Dickens and Dostoevsky, Jane Austen, Lewis Carroll, Henry James, Thackeray. But how many now read and are intimate with Hazlitt, Lamb, Matthew Arnold, Chesterton, Izaak Walton, Horace Walpole, Ruskin, Spenser, Robert Bridges or Sir Thomas Browne, outside small corners of academia? It would have been taken for granted that an educated man like David Cecil would know them all. I wonder when that ceased to be the case.

# A Book by its Cover

MY HUSBAND WAS once given the most extraordinary – I cannot really say book, it was more an artefact or a piece of sculpture. It did contain print on paper and it was bound, but any resemblance to what you would usually think of when you use the word 'book' ended there.

It was a copy of Shakespeare's *Hamlet*. It was a couple of feet tall and the front was made of stone or possibly marble, with a bas-relief sculpture of the artist's vision of the play's inner meaning. It weighed several pounds, it came from Italy, and there were only a handful like it; all were to be given to libraries except for one, which was a gift to the actor Sir John Gielgud, and this, which sat on our kitchen table looking impressive, important and odd. We had no idea what to do with it because it was not a book that could be read nor was it, to our eyes, an attractive object. It was a hybrid thing and it was eventually presented to some library. I wonder if they were glad of it. Books like that are collector's pieces, bought for their bindings alone. They often have little to do with reading and nor do leather bindings, however beautifully tooled in pretty colours. Some of the people who have row upon row of leather-bound books are owners of ancestral libraries in stately homes, but, although they can be very impressive to look at, those rooms of towering shelves always seem dead. Nobody would dare turn down a corner of a page or make a mark in any margin.

The Folio Society's *raison d'être* is fine binding, though of a mass-produced kind. The books are beautifully printed on good quality paper, illustrated by specially commissioned contemporary artists, and the bindings are always striking, never fuddy-duddy, and each one comes in a stout slip case. They look good on the shelves, and the older ones were covered in real cloth which is more pleasing to handle than the synthetic of more recent titles. Yet there is something dead about them, too, something too perfect, pro-duced for display rather than use. There are perhaps a couple of dozen of them scattered about the house, mainly odd volumes of Trollope, with a copy of *Cranford* and an Edgar Allen Poe thrown in, but these have been parted from their slip cases, read, handled. They would not pass muster among people who dust their books every week but they give pleasure nevertheless. But I would suspect anyone who had shelf after shelf of them, probably in alphabetical order, of not being a proper reader.

Dust jackets are another matter. To publishers, jackets are second only to content in importance – in some cases they may even come first. 'A good selling cover' is a thing to be desired in the trade and many a book has sold fewer copies than it deserved because of the wrong jacket. They should not have the power and influence they do – but they do.

I do cherish some of my books for their covers – Virginia Woolf with the Vanessa Bell covers, the Nonesuch Dickens with the original illustrations on the front, the early Ian Flemings.

I have occasionally bought a book as an investment because I would rather put my money into them than into stocks and shares and, just as you can always drink a cellar of fine wine if the bottom drops out of the market, you can always read a book (and read it again and again, which is more than can be said of the wine).

Some years ago a friend had a salutary lesson in the importance of dust jackets which has made me take more care of those I know to be of some value. He had a serious collection of first editions of twentieth-century poetry, including all of T.S. Eliot, and of first editions of E.M. Forster, D.H. Lawrence, Virginia Woolf and some others of equal rank. He also owned some fine private press books – *The Chaucer Head*, *Kelmscott*. He liked to look, to handle and to read his books but he was always careful not to mark or damage them. He did, however, have a dislike of dust jackets which he regarded rather like brown paper bags for groceries or envelopes containing letters. He thought they were of no interest or significance and he preferred the bindings they concealed. So he simply tore them off as soon as he bought his books and threw them away.

Then he came to me for advice. He needed money to help pay for his youngest son's education and proposed to sell some of his book collection. Did I know of a good dealer who would give him a fair price? I did. My friend compiled a list of what he wished to sell and sent it down. The dealer proposed an immediate visit. First editions of *The Four Quartets*, *The Waste Land*, *A Passage to India*, *A Room with a View*, *To the Lighthouse*, as well as a juicy selection of private press volumes, do not come the way of an antiquarian bookseller every day of the week.

He arrived and was shown the private press books first. He named a good price. Then they crossed the room to the Modern Firsts.

When he saw the rows of them, immaculate and in near-fine condition but every single one without its dust jacket, he wept, and when he heard that these had been torn off and thrown away, he wept again. The books were worth something, of course, but with their original near-mint dust jackets they would have been worth ten times as much. My friend was flabbergasted – indeed, for a while, he was disbelieving, so that the dealer suggested he ask a colleague to reinforce what he had said. They contacted him by phone and my friend spoke to him, only to hear the same story. The rest of the money for his son's education had to be found some other way.

But I don't think the moral of the story is to wrap all your books in cellophane and handle them, if at all, wearing gloves. My friend continued to enjoy his books. He got *The Waste Land* and *The Four Quartets* by heart from them, he read his Forster and Woolf many times before he died and when he did, his son had them to enjoy. I once asked if he regretted having to sell his private press books. He said he had barely noticed their absence. 'They were handsome objects', he said, 'but they were not books.'

# Roots

WHEN I HAD MONEY to buy rather than borrow books, each one had to justify itself, in terms of financial outlay but also in terms of space in the bookcase of my first flat. But I knew I would want more. The advance on royalties for my first book was put into trust for me until I was twenty-one and as soon as I got access to it I bought a bookcase. It was made for me by the generous father of a friend (all I had to pay for was the wood), and he measured and fitted it carefully to fill the whole of one wall. That bookcase moved with me from my first to my second flat, then to a house and even came with me into married life, moving twice before finally being left behind when no wall in a sixteenth-century cottage could accommodate it.

At first, there were a lot of empty spaces, filled with odd photographs and vases, but gradually the books took over, especially once I started reviewing them. The first books I bought were plays – dozens of plays, some classic drama by writers such as Ibsen, Chekhov, Webster, but far more modern plays, by Arthur Miller,

Ionesco, Tennessee Williams, Eugene O'Neill and then Pinter, David Storey, Shelagh Delaney and Arnold Wesker. I was far more interested in the theatre than anything else. That was a legacy of my early years in Scarborough, when my mother had taken me to the Repertory Theatre every other week from an age when I was far too young to appreciate most of the plays we saw and yet not too young to be excited by the magic of the theatrical experience. Those were the great days of rep, and the company alternated between Scarborough and York, putting on great plays, even Shakespeare, as well as all sorts of middlebrow, middle-class stuff from Agatha Christie to Emlyn Williams, Noel Coward and Terence Rattigan and that great old rep standby, *The Holly and the Ivy*. I saw Sheridan and Oscar Wilde, *The Browning Version*, *The Deep Blue Sea*, *Design for Living*, *Blithe Spirit* … I wonder what my eight-year-old self made of them? But whole scenes, particular actors, are still vivid in my mind. From there, it was only a move across town to Stephen Joseph's Theatre in the Round, which began in an upstairs space at the Scarborough Public Library. That was to play an even bigger part in my life years later, when it was headed by Alan Ayckbourn, and an actor-cum-writer Stephen Mallatratt had an idea for adapting my ghost story, *The Woman in Black*, to be performed there as an 'extra' alongside the pantomime, one Christmas.

Long before then, my family moved from Scarborough to Coventry, then a city having a great renaissance of rebuilding and a huge injection of life and hope after its devastation during the Second World War. When we arrived there in 1958, the Belgrade Theatre – the Civic Theatre – had just been built and opened. I was sixteen and stage-struck. I went there the week after we arrived, to enrol at the Saturday morning club called the Young Stagers.

We had talks from visiting playwrights, directors and actors, went backstage, did workshops – and then were invited to submit our own short plays which would be produced by one of the theatre team, but acted by Young Stagers themselves. I wrote a play, in the evenings after A-level homework. It was put on. I saw a glittering career as a playwright ahead of me – one which was never to materialise. But it was a heady time. The Belgrade gave first acting jobs to many who went on to become important names in the British theatre, Ian McKellen and Trevor Nunn among them.

It also saw the first performances of Arnold Wesker's early plays and, in particular, the *Roots* trilogy, which went from there to the Royal Court Theatre, London, and round the world. I went to every one of the Wesker first nights and, during the school holidays, I got a two-pounds-a-week job at the Belgrade as a general factotum, which was how I got to know Arnold and his wife Dusty, and how, when I went up to King's, I spent happy evenings babysitting for their small children. Anyone looking at the history of the British theatre, and at the history of Britain in the 1960s, will find Arnold Wesker there among the so-called Angry Young Men. There are plenty of other names, too – Lindsay Anderson, John Osborne, director John Dexter – and other places – the Royal Court, the Round House. It seems a lifetime away now but living through it and in it was incredibly exciting.

The legacy of those days is here in a small row of paperbacks in the Penguin Modern Drama series, with a few Faber plays thrown in. Here are the Wesker plays, here is Shelagh Delaney's *A Taste of Honey*, here are Osborne and Pinter. I have not looked at any of them for years. Something happened. The theatre died on me. Why? How? I had wanted to be a playwright ever since that time.

I still do. I never will be. It is the hardest form of writing, I am convinced of that, and one I was never going to master. (The stage adaptation of my ghost story *The Woman in Black* was brilliantly done by Stephen Mallatratt and the adapter's skill is another I wish I possessed.) At the back of cupboards are notebooks with half-written plays and ideas for plays. I went on scratching away at the itch for years.

But I have never stopped finding things in plays that I have never found in the novel and so, although I rarely go to the theatre, I sometimes read plays, and when I do, I find elements that I missed when watching a performance. The dialogue flits by, the scene changes, so much is lost. David Hare is a playwright I have admired more than any other and I have re-read *Racing Demon* and *Skylight* and *Amy's View* until I know them by heart. There is so much depth in them and yet there are so few words. Hare goes through most human emotions in a small space.

These dramas are old friends and when I read the character lists and the names of the actors in the first performances, they open windows on to my past, a youth when I was stage-struck and star-struck. We all were.

A few years ago I was speaking at the Hay Book Festival and staying for a day or two in that pretty town; but it gets hideously crowded so after my talk, rather than try to eat in a packed café, I went down to the delicatessen to buy a sandwich. The shop was busy. I hovered, wondering whether to queue. And then I saw him. Yes? No? Of course, it was. Arnold Wesker is Arnold Wesker. He was unchanged – just a little older.

'Excuse me – are you Arnold Wesker?'

'Sometimes.' Which was exactly the sort of thing Arnold would have said. He turned round to me, and his hug gathered together all the threads of our shared past, forty-five years ago.

When I came home, I took down his plays and read them again. They have never received the appreciation they deserve in this country, though they were highly successful all over Europe from the beginning. They are unlikely to be performed much in Britain now, partly because repertory theatre no longer exists, partly because they have large casts and numerous elaborate sets and so cost a prohibitive amount to stage, but more because they are very much of their time, and that time has not yet become all-time. But if we want to know about post-war life in Britain, about what people's aspirations and fears were, how they lived and related to one another in a bleak new order which was yet full of all kinds of political and personal hope – hope which has never really been fulfilled – then we should study Wesker's plays. They are rich and vibrant with articulate human life and dreams; they do not have the bareness of Pinter or the bitterness of Osborne. Wesker was always full of anger, righteous anger, but he was never a bitter writer and cynicism is the very last thing you find in his work. It is full of the warmth and energy and extraordinary life-experience of the man.

Does it matter that it would be hard to find a production of the plays? No, because they read so well, no, because the reader's imagination liberates them from what I see as, ultimately, a confining art – the drama. The reader's imagination can supply every character, every setting, every vocal nuance. Theatre sometimes does these things itself – as Shakespeare says in the opening chorus to *Henry V*. A whole battlefield can be presented by a handful of actors within the confines of the 'Wooden O' so long as the audience is prepared to participate imaginatively by filling in the gaps. That is how Stephen Mallatratt was able to transform a ghost story with swirling London fog, busy railway stations, an isolated house across a causeway, a bustling marketplace not on to film, but into the same 'Wooden O' with two actors and a few props. The audience supplies the rest. But *The Woman in Black* is an adaptation of a novel. Most plays were written for performance in a theatre alone. Yet I still find that almost all of them yield as much, if not more, to the silent and solitary reader who can go back and re-read a line or two, pause and think, work out slowly and carefully what exactly is happening and the meaning of what is being said. Only bad playwrights cannot stand up to such close scrutiny.

# Slow, Slow, Slow-Slow, Slow

ALTHOUGH WHEN I was a child and growing up I could borrow books every week from the library, there was a limit on the number to be taken at any one time and so, as there was not the money to buy many books either, I found myself reading, re-reading and re-reading again. If I liked a library book I simply got to the end, turned it round and began it again. It was a bit like sweets. Until I was ten, sweets were rationed. I had a quarter of a pound a week and there were various ways in which they could be made to last. One sweet a day. Buy only boiled sweets which could be sucked for a long time. Suck half and re-wrap the rest until tomorrow. Occasionally I would have such a sugar-craving that I bought something that was gobbled up in a great burst of sweetness that exploded in the mouth like a firework and then was gone. Sherbet lemons were like that. Marshmallows did not last long.

On the whole, I preferred to buy fruit drops and suck them slowly to extract every last bit of flavour and sweetness over as long a period as possible. It was the same with books, and although my attitude to sweets may have shifted, it is the same with books now.

When people had only the Bible and the Prayer Book to read, they read them every day, knew them from front to back and in reverse, and for reasons that were not only religious. Whatever your beliefs, the Bible is full of good stories, magnificently told. I am uncertain if I could go for a year without anything else but it would be interesting to see what it was like to have only the Bible and the Book of Common Prayer to read, slowly and carefully, for a month.

A strange competitiveness has emerged among some readers in the last few years. I have known book-bloggers boast of getting through twenty books plus, a week, as if they were trying for a place in the *Guinness Book of Records*. Why has reading turned into a form of speed dating? And then there is fashion and the desire to have the very latest book – which doesn't matter a scrap so long as the book is wanted for itself, not just because it is the one everybody is talking about, and so long as plenty of other, unfashionable books are desired as well.

Some years ago, magazines carried adverts for correspondence courses that taught speed reading, a useful skill for those who have to digest a great deal of information quickly – lawyers, perhaps. But lawyers read material that does not have to be retained for long, and is not of great literary or artistic merit.

The best books deserve better. Everything I am reading during this year has so much to yield but only if I give it my full attention and respect it by reading it slowly. Fast reading of a great novel will get us the plot. It will get us names, a shadowy idea of characters, a sketch of settings. It will not get us subtleties, small differentiations, depth of emotion and observation, multilayered human experience, the appreciation of simile and metaphor, any sense of context, any comparison with other novels, other writers. Fast reading will not get us cadence and complexities of style and language. It will not get us anything that enters not just the conscious mind but the unconscious. It will not allow the book to burrow down into our memory and become part of ourselves, the accumulation of knowledge and wisdom and vicarious experience which helps to form us as complete human beings. It will not develop our awareness or add to the sum of our knowledge and intelligence. Read parts of a newspaper quickly or an encyclopaedia entry, or a fast-food thriller, but do not insult yourself or a book which has been created with its author's painstakingly acquired skill and effort, by seeing how fast you can dispose of it.

Slow reading is deeply satisfying. I read two or three chapters of *To the Lighthouse*, or *Little Dorrit*, or *The Age of Innocence* or *Midnight's Children*, and stop, go back, look at how the sentences and paragraphs are put together, how the narrative works, how a character is brought to life. But I want to think about what I have read before I move on for only in this way will I appreciate the whole as being both the sum of, and more than the sum of, its parts.

There is a Slow Movement of which slow reading occupies only a tiny corner – one that has not become as widely known, recommended or practised as Slow Food. I wish it would.

I do not read as much poetry as I should but I do re-read it – Chaucer, George Herbert, Vaughan, Donne, Auden, Hardy, T.S. Eliot, Seamus Heaney, Ted Hughes, Charles Causley – the poets who have stood by me through thick and thin over many years. There is more than enough there to last me for the rest of my life. It is in the nature of poetry to demand slow reading before it will yield anything apart from, occasionally, a jolly rhyme and rhythm. You can read 'The Lady of Shalott' or 'The Ballad of John Gilpin' fast – they gather speed and carry you along and there isn't much more to them than that. But how could you take in the smallest sliver of meaning from *The Four Quartets* by reading them in that way? How could Henry James yield a one-hundredth of his meaning or any of the subtleties of his style other than through a slow reading?

Not every book is worth that sort of effort – who pretends that it is? A comic novel, a fast-paced thriller demand little and their reward is immediate – they are ice-cream reading, and barely a trace of the flavour remains half an hour after they are finished. Sometimes, only ice cream will do. But we are not nourished physically, mentally, artistically or spiritually by its literary equivalent.

I wonder what it would be like to have just forty books left to read for the rest of my life. I have a made a mental bookshelf. It is empty now but I am going to place on it the forty books I think I could manage with alone, for the rest of my life – if push came to shove.

Forty books.

I will not even make the *Desert Island Discs* assumption that the Bible and Shakespeare are already in situ. Even those will have to earn their place.

Where shall I begin?

Not with the Bible but with the 1662 Book of Common Prayer. It is small but it contains everything I may need to nourish me spiritually, and to be a living stream of linguistic glory from which I can drink and be refreshed every day. The Collects and the Psalms are here, and the Orders for Morning and Evening Prayer, and everywhere I open the book I find words that echo from my past. I heard these words at Coventry Cathedral, week in, week out, and became steeped in them, and though I never consciously learned any of them by heart, they are there nevertheless, reminding me of the place and people at the most formative time of any in my life. The Psalms often come to mind with accompanying music too. 'Like as the Hart','O Clap your Hands', 'O be Joyful in God all Ye Lands', 'Many Waters Cannot Quench Love'. The seasons come and go with the Collects, including one I especially like: 'Stir up, we beseech Thee O Lord, the wills of Thy faithful people; that they, plenteously bringing forth the fruit of good works, may of Thee be plenteously rewarded.' That is the Collect for the Twenty-Fifth Sunday after Trinity, which used to be known as 'Stir-up Sunday' not only because of the opening words but because people traditionally stirred their Christmas puddings on that day.

If the Bible and Book of Common Prayer are part of the warp and woof of your upbringing, the words gather meanings to themselves over years, personal meanings, associative meanings, odd meanings. You could be illiterate but, by going to church and hearing these words every week, have more riches in heart and mind than many who know how to read but read little of lasting value or significance.

So the cornerstone of my final library of just forty books is the 1662 Prayer Book and, although small versions with India paper are easy to slip into the pocket and stack nicely on the ends of pews, the best edition for reading is in the new Everyman's Library, so that is the one I will keep.

The Bible earns its place in the King James's version because of the language, which is as much part of me as that of the Prayer Book, though the New Revised Standard Version is probably a better translation and almost – but only almost – as graceful. About ten years ago I read the Bible all the way through, from soup to nuts, not even skipping the long lists of Kings and the structural engineering instructions for the building of the Temple, and it struck me that, firstly, it is packed full of good stories no matter what your beliefs or lack of them, secondly, that it contains so much that is and will always be pertinent to the human condition, and thirdly, that the Christian faith really is rooted in the Old Testament, and therefore in Judaism. I have a strong sense of kinship with all Jews, and Jewish prayers and services seem to have far more to say to me, as a Christian, than those of any other religions, which are alien, no matter how interesting. But with Judaism I am at home. The Old and the New Testaments – or the Hebrew Bible and the New Testament, as we are sometimes urged to say – are two halves of a whole and the second flows out of the first. I wish more people remembered that.

So there are my first two, and Shakespeare must be on the shelf because I want to read him, not see him performed, but so as not to cause dissent in the home I will steer clear of all modern versions and plump for the old familiar Alexander edition. But the inclusion of a *Complete Shakespeare* leads to the argument that this is not one book but many. If I am to play strictly by the rules then I may take just one book containing one work. Ah, the old parlour game. Right, we shall play it. From Shakespeare, I will not keep:

Any of the poetry.

Any of the Roman plays.

A History play? Possibly. *Henry IV Part 1* goes down on the longlist. Then come the Tragedies. *Macbeth* is exciting. *King Lear* is depressing. *Othello* is a most annoying play … Of those three, *Macbeth* stays, for now. *Hamlet*, definitely. Exciting, dense and

rich, varied, fast-paced scenes alternating with slower ones and
a great ghost story … If it is between *Macbeth* and *Hamlet* then
there is no contest. Or is there? *Macbeth* is one of the great crime
stories of the world and has arguably the best villainess in literature. Both stay in for now.

The Comedies next, and *Twelfth Night* and *As You Like It* go out at
once, as does *The Comedy of Errors*. *A Midsummer Night's Dream*
must stay.

Then come what we called the 'Problem Plays', though I gather the
term has fallen out of favour in academia, and out of those I
think I'll keep *All's Well that Ends Well* because it is strange and
interesting. Of the late plays, *The Tempest* has to stay. It may be
my favourite play.

So, we have a shortlist of *Henry IV Part One*, *Hamlet*, *Macbeth*,
*A Midsummer Night's Dream*, *All's Well* and *The Tempest* and many
people would find that an odd selection and wouldn't dream of
abandoning several of the others – but the arguments are half the
fun of the game.

*Henry IV* has to go because one history play by itself does not
quite work, and *A Midsummer Night's Dream* goes too, because,
although so much of it is magical, the lovers' knots are very tiresome and Theseus and Hippolyta are dull. Do I knock out *Macbeth*
or *Hamlet*? Pass for the moment. *All's Well* versus *The Tempest*. No
contest. *The Tempest* stays. Three in the ring. Help. I can't do this.
Yes. I can, it's easy. I know *Hamlet* so well that if I absolutely had
to, I could probably sit down and recite quite a lot of it but I
couldn't say the same of *Macbeth*, apart from what you might call
the quotations. I'll keep *Macbeth*.

The final choice? This is the *only* Shakespeare play I am allowed to keep and read for the rest of my life, unless I use up a precious second book out of my forty.

I am going to leave the decision to mature until later.

Some would call this business downsizing, others de-cluttering. I think I will call it 'crystallising'.

# Long Barn

I LOVE THE BOOK. I love the feel of a book in my hands, the compactness of it, the shape, the size. I love the feel of paper. The sound it makes when I turn a page. I love the beauty of print on paper, the patterns, the shapes, the fonts. I am astonished by the versatility and practicality of The Book. It is so simple. It is so fit for its purpose. It may give me mere content, but no e-reader will ever give me that sort of added pleasure.

I grew up loving both books and The Book, and having spent so many years reading and writing them I suppose it was inevitable that one day I would want to make them and publish them. It's a bug that gets to quite a few people. I could feel myself moving inexorably towards becoming a publisher for several years but it was a very slow, semi-conscious movement. And then several things happened within a short space of time to make the last moves very swift.

I met Roy Strong on Paddington Station and as we waited for our trains we spoke of this and that, in the course of which he told

me that he was wondering whether or not to publish his diaries. I
urged him to do just that. And I suddenly heard myself telling him
that I was wondering whether or not to start a small publishing
company.

'If you publish your diaries, I'll buy them,' I said.

'If you start a publishing company, I'll do a book for you,' he
said, and then he added, 'Do it. We should all embark on something completely new every ten years. And besides, it will be fun.'

Roy published his diaries. In my copy he wrote 'To Susan, who
enters my life at significant moments.' Well, so does he.

Meanwhile, he had started me thinking.

I knew who I wanted to emulate, of course. Virginia Woolf, that
practical woman who, with Leonard, decided to launch the Hogarth
Press and so bought a printing press, which was delivered into their
dining room along with a manual on how to work it. I thought back
to the Christmas I had received my equivalent, the John Bull Printing Set. No one who missed the era of the John Bull Printing Set
can say they have lived. The set consisted of a cardboard box containing small wooden racks and strips of rubber letters, together
with a few numbers and punctuation marks, tweezers, an ink-pad
and stamp. You carefully split the rubber strips and removed each
letter with the tweezers, a most fiddly job, and set it out on the
rack. When you had formed two or three words to make a sentence,
you transferred the words one at a time to the slots in the stamp –
and, of course, everything was in mirror language and had to be
inserted backwards. Then you pressed the stamp with its word on
to the ink-pad and when it was nicely coated, stamped it on to
paper. Invariably, you either pressed too hard, took up too much ink
and made a blobby word, or you pressed too lightly and made a

faint word, or only a part of it. It was a tricky and delicate operation. The other risks were forgetting to put the letters in backwards order so that your words came out as lluB nhoJ. Or sometimes, luBl Jonh. To make an entire sentence, even with patience and practice, by trial and error, took ages. The most common accident was, of course, the dropping of the box which, like buttered toast, always turned upside down so that little rubber letters went everywhere, to be eaten by the dog or the vacuum cleaner and never seen again.

I started several newspapers using my John Bull, and even one or two books, but in the end it was clear that the operation was too fraught with technical difficulties to succeed and that my manual dexterity left much to be desired, so although I continued writing, editing and publishing newspapers, albeit with a small circulation, they were handwritten. They all folded eventually.

But the charm of the John Bull Printing Set was still considerable because for a short time it seemed to lift me nearer to the worlds of printing and publishing, which fascinated me even then. The delight was fed when I went to King's, and I often walked up into Fleet Street to see the printing presses thunder out the daily papers. During the final summer between school and university I had a job as a cub reporter on a local paper and went to watch my first article being typeset in the old way. The principle was pretty much the same as with the John Bull – trays of letters set in mirror language, great containers of ink, the finished sentences and paragraphs pressed on to paper. The history of printing is both interesting and romantic. I wonder if Leonard and Virginia Woolf dropped all the letters on the dining-room carpet while they were mastering the art and starting to print Hogarth Press pamphlets, early poems by T.S. Eliot and stories by Katherine Mansfield. On my Woolf and

Bloomsbury shelves, I have a complete list of Hogarth Press publications, and it has been my inspiration. From time to time I just take it down and browse the titles, *pour encourager*.

Perhaps the desire to be a publisher was always there, ever since the John Bull Printing Set days. It was the remark of Roy Strong's about embarking on something new every ten years that was the real spur.

But where to begin? How do you publish a book? How do you start a publishing company?

If in doubt, practise on yourself. I did not want to become a self-publisher – that is something different, and I already had several publishers for my own books. But then I remembered the short stories. Penelope Fitzgerald once told me how astonished she was to discover that a lot of writers had drawers full of short stories. It astonished me, too. Short stories have always been as rare as hen's teeth in this house. But something strange had happened a year previously, when I had had a brush with death, survived, and, as a result, felt as if bits of my unconscious had floated to the surface, like debris after a storm. In among the bits had been four short stories, which I had written one after the other, quite urgently, as if afraid that they might sink back to the depths of the ocean again. But four stories do not a volume make, and I had put them away in a drawer, hoping that eventually I would have more to make up a collection.

I took them out, re-read them, tidied them up a bit. Here was what I could begin with – a small book of short stories, a modest paperback. I had my own name to trade on, as it were, which gave me a head start, but after that I had nothing.

I did not even have a name for the company. The Hogarth Press was called after the house in Richmond in which the Woolfs were living. Our house name would not quite work. But across the yard from the main house is a fine old barn, a long barn with three open arches at the front. One night I looked out of my bedroom window and saw it in the moonlight. 'Long Barn' I thought, and then added 'Books'. Bingo. The next day I opened Virginia Woolf's *A Writer's Diary* at an entry which read 'Just back from staying with Vita at Long Barn.' If I had needed a sign, there it was.

Publishing has been a hugely enjoyable sideline to writing my own books and it has taught me a very great deal about the other side of the business. I now understand why certain things have to happen the way they do, even though authors are not pleased by them. I know how much time, trouble, thought and financial risk go into making and bringing out a book. I know how difficult it is to sell books. My respect for my fellow publishers has soared.

And here are the Long Barn Books: Ronald Blythe's essays, *Going to Meet George and Other Outings*; Debo Devonshire's hilarious collection of pieces about life at Chatsworth, life in the country, and the madnesses of the world, *Counting my Chickens*; Quentin Crewe's travel book, *Letters from India*; Nick Peto's scurrilous, side-achingly funny autobiography, *Peto's Progress*; Tom Parker Bowles's first book, *E is for Eating*, with its zingy cover and quirky illustrations by Matthew Rice. Here is *William Shakespeare: The Quiz Book* by Stanley Wells, illustrated by John Lawrence's woodcuts, and with the answer booklet printed separately and slipped into a pocket at the back so that if you are the sort of person who cheats at quizzes, you can remove it before attempting them. And then, inevitably, lose it. Knowing that this would happen, we offered a free replacement booklet on receipt of a stamp. Paddy Leigh Fermor got through four replacements, and because he lives in Greece for most of the year and does not have our stamps, sent me a cheque for £1. I never cashed it, of course. Whoever would bank a cheque for one pound, signed by Patrick Leigh Fermor?

I am proud of every book, proud to have made books as well as written them. Roy Strong was right and I am glad I learned something new in the last decade of the twentieth century. Publishing *is* a lot of fun and I bet Leonard and Virginia thought so, too. And so long as there are readers there will be publishers, and so long as there are both there will be books, real books, printed on paper and bound into volumes. I will put money on it.

# The Way we Live Now

I HAVE NOT FORGOTTEN the look of scorn that froze on the features of one particular English tutor when I mentioned that I was reading Trollope. It is hard to understand that attitude now, but it was not uncommon. The great Victorian novelists were Dickens, George Eliot, the Brontës, perhaps Thackeray. Trollope was thought of by many academics as a pen-pusher, who self-confessedly churned books out to a strict daily timetable, while working for the Post Office. I inherited this sort of intellectual snobbery and for a few years believed that real creative writers waited for inspiration and when it came, honed their few sentences like guardsmen shining their boots. Writing fiction was not regarded as something you did as a set task at a set time every day, let alone with a regular target of words. Those who saw things this way had never, of course, tried either and certainly never had to work to a deadline, let alone earn a living by writing. Yet Dickens published his books in parts – he was effectively a magazine writer in the first instance, and had to work whether or not he felt inspired to do so on any given day. Nobody has ever sneered at Dickens in the way people sneered at Trollope and I have often wondered what it is about him that provoked such derision, other than his working habits. Perhaps those who sneered did not stay to read. People do take up positions over books as over anything else, and stick to them wrong-headedly and stubbornly, on the flimsiest of evidence.

I first read Trollope for A level when we studied *The Warden*. I found it beguiling but melancholy and inevitably, after three terms of close analysis of what is a relatively slight novel, plus essays and exams on it, too, I wearied of it and did not feel interested enough to take up the next in the series. I came to the rest of the Barsetshire novels much later, when I was no longer prejudiced against reading more about clergymen. Before that, I read my way through the political novels and I did so, like many other people, because of the television adaptation in the early 1970s. *The Pallisers*, as the series was called, is not merely golden in the memory, it is one of the great television dramatisations in the history of that medium, and I say so having watched every episode again in the last year in the immaculately re-originated DVD version. So often, what we remember as great television later seems slow, over-acted and, in the case of comedy, no longer funny. But *The Pallisers* is enthralling, the acting some of the best I have seen on the small screen, the period detail flawless. After I watched them all again, I went back to the books, and the faces and voices of the dramatisation stayed in my mind – the faces of Roger Livesey, a young Anna Massey and the beautiful Susan Hampshire, the face of a perfectly cast Philip Latham as Plantagenet and those of others, long dead or vanished from our screens – these are still the faces I see as I read, down to the very young Anthony Andrews and Jeremy Irons as two of the Duke's children.

But there is more to Trollope than there is to, say, *The Forsyte Saga*, a television dramatisation of the 1960s. There is a depth of human understanding, a political insight and wisdom, a perceptiveness of how men behave in public and again in private life, and how one influences and supports the other. Trollope understands the nature of power – how it is used best and how it can corrupt. He understands the machinations of men who long for power, the wheeling and dealing involved in the political game, the nature of deception. He was an observer, as all the best realistic novelists have been, not an insider, and so he is able to make revelations, to strip away pretensions with a fine scalpel, to probe to the heart of a man, or the motives for an action. What he says about the political world, and the social worlds that revolve in its orbit, is as relevant today as it was in his own time, and so long as a parliamentary democracy continues to work in the same way it will continue to be so.

Trollope is a past master both at handling a great many characters within the novel, and in driving his narrative lines clearly forward. Dickens was a master at handling a large number of characters, too, but, probably because he was writing under pressure, part by part, his narrative line is sometimes confused and there are often discrepancies – though they never seem to matter, so swept on is the reader by the whole great performance. But Trollope has a cooler head.

He is also more of a realist. Dickens has pantomime villains and bizarre grotesques, sentimental heroines and pasteboard heroes. His scenes are great tableaux, strung together. Trollope's characters are such as you might have met every day if you had moved in the worlds of politics and great houses, parishes and Victorian cathedral closes. He creates detailed and wholly believable worlds. Sometimes he is pedestrian, especially in the many minor Irish novels. But he is such an intricate writer, subtle in his observations, multifaceted as the societies he lays bare. The tutor who sneered at him as lightweight can surely not have read his masterpiece, *The Way we Live Now*. I have read critics describe Trollope as missing greatness, without the genius touch of Dickens, but *The Way we Live Now* is a masterpiece by any literary standards, Melmotte one of the great evil men of fiction – ruthless, cold, cruel, manipulative, vain, cunning – and wholly believable. Dickens could have created him but he would have done so very differently. Dickens's Victorian world is odd, slightly distorted – we see scenes and characters as if in one of those fairground mirrors which make some things elephantine, some elongated, others dwarfish. Dickens liked grotesques and some of his novels have the quality of nightmare, almost surrealist in effect. This is so far away from Trollope that we might be looking at a different age. Henry James wrote that 'there are two kinds of taste in the appreciation of imaginative literature: the taste for emotions of surprise and the taste for emotions of recognition. It is the latter that Trollope gratifies.'

Dickens for one view, Trollope for another, Dickens for one reading-mood, Trollope for its counterpart. I would not want to be without either. My tutor was wrong about Trollope because he was reading him, as it were, with the wrong expectations, through the wrong lenses. Adjust the view and he comes into sharp focus.

My fiction shelves are not laden with Victorian novels but they seem thick with both Dickens and Trollope, and my forty books cannot contain very many of either. I go to the Dickens shelf and run my hand along the various editions, taking out several and discarding them, leaving a crystallisation again. What is left? *Little Dorrit. Bleak House. Great Expectations. A Christmas Carol. Our Mutual Friend.* The *Carol* can go because I know it so well I scarcely need it, and *Great Expectations*, because it is short and I must make each volume pay its way by the pound and the spine width as well as by the quality. My Dickens has to be *Our Mutual Friend*.

But Trollope is harder because how can I take one Barchester Chronicle, one political novel? Do any of them stand alone? I think *The Last Chronicle of Barset* does, and it is a mighty novel. It is the culmination and the crown of them. None of the political novels can be detached from its fellows in the same way without suffering damage. Then, bleak and dark though it is, and lacking the well-loved characters who walk through Barsetshire or stroll among the politicians and the Dukes and Duchesses as it does, I have to bring it down to the best and keep *The Way we Live Now* on my shelf.

I have spent a long time among the Victorians this winter but the year is on the turn, the first spring crocuses are pushing up through the grass. It is not yet warm, there are no leaves on the trees but just perceptibly the nights are drawing out.

I am restless for the twentieth century again. Upstairs then, to the landing. Why Forster sits next to Graham Greene, or Anita Brookner is tucked in beside V.S. Naipaul, let alone why they are interspersed with odd volumes of the *Finn Family Moomintroll*, is one of the mysteries of the reading life.

I put my hand out, bypassing the Moomins just for now, and, as it rests on *A House for Mr Biswas*, I have a flash of recall: V.S. Naipaul entering through the door of the BBC Radio 4 studio for an interview with me on *Bookshelf*. It is 1987 and pride comes before a fall. When he comes up to me and takes my hand in his silken ones, he bows.

'I am most *honoured* to meet …' a pause. Then '… the wife of the distinguished Shakespeare scholar Stanley Wells.'

It is difficult to put the second half of the twentieth century together with the first when trying to arrange novelists into a tentative order of greatness. Many would say it is a pointless task, but there are levels of achievement, in this as in anything else: there are the great and the ordinary, and time helps us to see the great more clearly as the rest fall away. We need a mark against which to measure greatness, but the first half of the twentieth century contains some novelists who have not so far been surpassed, and some who really belong with the Victorians. Thomas Hardy is the obvious example of the latter, but so is another great, and greatly underestimated novelist, Arnold Bennett.

But there is surely no novelist writing since the 1950s who is greater than Naipaul. He is a complex thinker, a magnificent prose writer, a painter on a broad canvas, able to portray not just a place but a continent and a philosophy, a history and a civilisation. Yet he is always clear, always readable, deep but never obscure, which surely adds to the measure of his achievement – almost all the best novelists can be read by the interested and committed reader. However great a writer is – Proust, say, or James Joyce – the fact that so very many willing and intelligent readers find them difficult, even impenetrable, is surely a mark, albeit in pencil, against them. This is not a plea for an 'easy read' – concentration, focus and application are necessary in direct proportion to the richness and depth of a text, and bring their own reward. But linguistic or stylistic obscurity is a hindrance to understanding. V.S. Naipaul's prose, by contrast, is supple and clear, his vocabulary huge, and his manipulation of language masterly. He is able to make us laugh and cry and marvel within a couple of sentences, and packs in a wealth of multifaceted meaning and reference.

> The exchange took place on the back steps and reached the ears of Mr Biswas, lying in pants and vest on the Slumberking bed in the room which contained most of the possessions he had gathered after forty-one years. He had carried on a war with Suniti ever since she was a child but his contempt had never been able to quell her sarcasm.
>
> 'Shama,' he shouted. 'Tell that girl to go back and help that worthless husband of hers look after their goats at Pokima Halt.'
>
> The goats were an invention of Mr Biswas which never failed to irritate Suniti. 'Goats!' she said to the yard, and sucked her teeth. 'Well, some people at least have goats. Which is more than I could say for some other people.'
>
> 'Tcha!' Mr Biswas said softly; and refusing to be drawn into an argument with Suniti, he turned on his side and continued to read the Meditations of Marcus Aurelius.

The last incongruity is typical of a novel whose whole identity, like that of its hero, Mohun Biswas, is bound up in incongruity. *A House for Mr Biswas* is a masterpiece which finds its way effortlessly on to my shelf. There is plenty more Naipaul dotted about the house and every volume adds to the sum of his stature but no one novel compares with *Mr Biswas*.

With Graham Greene, though, it is different. They are all here, as well as his *Collected Essays* and several books about him, of which my two favourites are Shirley Hazzard's delightful short book *Greene on Capri*, about a friendship formed during his later years, and the illuminating *The Other Man: Conversations with Graham Greene* by Marie-Françoise Allain. Greene straddles the twentieth century and I think he does so alone. There is no other novelist as good, writing over the same period. Many people reject some aspects of his work – his Catholicism, his anti-Americanism, but these do not detract from his greatness even if they are vital parts of his character and history. He gets under the skin of people so well, knows what makes them tick, especially in moral *extremis*, he understands and forgives and emphathises, he is clear-eyed, he can explain and apportion blame yet is always non-judgemental. His style is so straightforward, so lucid, so unshowy and yet it packs a massive punch.

But it was one of his essays, 'The Lost Childhood', which struck the loudest chord with me when I first read it, because there Greene puts his finger on what first spurred him to write – the books he read, and was so totally caught up in, as a child. The essay provoked an answering cry of recognition inside me. 'But that's how it was with me too!' When they come, however they come, those moments of spontaneous response are very significant.

I always longed to meet Greene, though I doubt if he would have had anything to say to me and many who did meet him found him difficult, tetchy, even dull. But I did once write to him.

In 1961 Greene's *A Burnt-Out Case* appeared on the same day as my first novel, and one of the popular newspapers, seeking to provoke, led with a long and flattering review of mine, while consigning Greene to a corner. It was an act of unpardonable rudeness, as well as bad judgement and, although my publisher was amused,

I felt mortified enough to write to Greene and apologise. Of course it was not my fault but it somehow felt as if it was. He wrote a most courteous and charming reply by hand. The letter has disappeared. I have longed for it to drop out of a Greene novel, or to find it stuck in some ancient notebook. When moving house or having a re-arrangement of books, I have made a thorough search for it and unearthed many another lost treasure. But never, alas, my letter from Graham Greene.

I must have one of his books among my forty and, because I am anxious for my collection to include humour and lightness, I am tempted to take *Travels with my Aunt*, or the wonderfully funny *Our Man in Havana*, about a vacuum-cleaner salesman, but perhaps they would pall. I dither between *The Quiet American*, *The End of the Affair* and *The Heart of the Matter*, eliminate the middle title, dither again. It has to be the greatest, I think, the most moving and, above all, that rarest of things, the novel which is entirely convincing about love. Graham Greene wrote about human love as well as Tolstoy and never better than in *The Heart of the Matter*, which is also so good at conveying the atmosphere, the heat, the squalor, the ennui of the West Africa he knew so well. So in it goes.

# Picture Books

ONE OF THE PLEASURES of reading aloud to small children is that you're also reading aloud to yourself. Many of the storybooks my daughters had are still here, battered and creased, well read and well loved, though many others flowed under the bridges, borrowed from the library, bought but never quite taken into the bosom of the family, as it were. The favourites were read aloud long after the children could read independently because the pleasures of being read to are many and carry on into adult life. Reading alone provides quite different literary pleasure. It is saddening to know that the majority of children never have stories read to them at home. How much they miss, of shared pleasure and fun, comfort and closeness, interest and learning. The children's books still left here are mainly paperbacks, apart from the pop-up books that is – but those are what used to be called Sunday Books, for careful page-turning with clean hands.

There is a strange assortment of the everyday, the fantastic, the simple and cheerful, the weird and the scary, and all were read, according to mood. The younger child liked nightmarish tales – a favourite was the Russian story of the witch with iron teeth, Baba Yaga – but the elder one had bad dreams and preferred gentler tales without too much sadness.

Beatrix Potter's small books with the shiny white jackets are here, masterpieces of observation and imagination. How comforting *Peter Rabbit* is, even though it is also a profoundly moral tale, and how realistically red in tooth and claw is *The Tale of Jemima Puddleduck*. Potter understood the countryside and there is not a trace of sentimentality in her. The stories are redolent of the Victorian nursery; rabbit and cat mothers speak kindly but firmly, and issue terrible warnings of the consequences of folly and misdeeds.

I have just gone through a shelf packed with picture books, and I find that most of the old favourites are a mixture of the ordinary and the odd and that many, chosen on a whim, stayed the course not because they are great children's literature – like Potter – but because they struck the right note at the right time, found favour and stood up to countless re-readings.

So familiar were they that they have become leitmotifs running through family life. They run still. The small boy James who cut his finger in the playground and felt, like the title, *Just Awful*, is remembered fondly whenever anybody in the family has to go to see the GP practice nurse; and one called Ben, who went fishing with his father, lives on every time anyone makes a tomato sandwich (which he used as unsuccessful bait). Nobody who forgets their manners can escape being reminded of Elfrida Vipont's *The Elephant and the Bad Baby* (who went 'Rumpeta, Rumpeta, Rumpeta, all down the road') – another moral tale. We take an animal to what is always referred to as the V.E.T. – because it was thought that Mog the

Forgetful Cat understood if you said the word aloud – and thinking of an owl inevitably means thinking either of *Meg and Mog* too, or of *The Owl who was Afraid of the Dark*.

Every family in which children are read to, and where books are part of the furniture and the reading of them part of life, must have its own mythology, one that has arisen out of early books. Characters become companions, they help form the imagination, they people a child's inner landscape. *Alice in Wonderland* and the White Rabbit, the Red Queen and the Caterpillar were far more to me than invented characters in a storybook. They still are. Looking at the children's picture books now, I realise that they are my books too, they became as much part of my inner landscape as of theirs. The best children's books defy age barriers though plenty of others do not move up with us into adulthood.

Enid Blyton served a purpose well but I doubt if I could last the course all the way through even one of them now, and I note how few are left on our shelves. Once outgrown, they have been given away with alacrity.

On a small bookcase in the hall I found a row of fiction which came after picture books. I wonder why they are still here, whether either girl would want them in future, if they hold sentimental memories, or none at all. There is a series about a girl called Ramona the Pest, another of horse and pony stories, and the much-loved Laura Ingalls Wilder books about the *Little House on the Prairie*. Others? *The House that Sailed Away*, *The Mona Lisa Mystery*, *The Worst Witch*, *Gobbolino the Witch's Cat*, *The Mouse and his Child* …

I take them out and put them back. One day, somebody will come upon them again and decide if they are wanted, but meanwhile, they take up little room and every one was once read and loved, which is the best reason for letting them stay here for a while longer.

A couple of years ago a friend of extremely left-wing and politically correct bent was looking at the shelf of children's books and remarked that they were all 'escapist'. She felt that my children had not been encouraged to engage in the gritty problems and troubles of real life through their reading. No, they had not. I always steered clear of 'issue literature' when choosing picture books for them – but then, there were few of that kind available for the under-fives in the 1970s and early 1980s, though occasionally there were titles aimed at helping children overcome a fear of dogs, for example, or the dentist. But she did not mean that sort of simple, helpful story. She was looking through the fiction they read between the ages of around eight to thirteen or so, before they moved on to adult novels. Escapist? I would call it imaginative. But if the lives of children in Elizabethan England, or a magical country called Narnia, and stories about creatures called Moomins are a means of escape from the often dull and tiresome everyday world, as well as being good books, what is the argument against that? Computer games are escapist, going to football matches or the cinema, or watching soaps or costume drama on television, are all forms of escapism. We need some.

Since our children's books were first bought, fiction for young readers has become more and more issue-led. Divorce, step-parents, drugs, alcohol, early sex, knife-crime, foster-care, child abuse, unemployment, gang warfare, AIDS, terminal illness … you name it, there is a novel for children about it. But all children are anxious, adult life contains much that is ugly and unhappy, unpleasant or downright bad. Why introduce them to that too early, through

books, which can be such a force for enjoyment, imaginative enrich-
ment, fun, excitement, adventure, magic? Realism comes home
soon enough and many children have too much anguish to cope
with in their everyday lives as it is. Their books can be one corner
of life that remains untainted by the troubles brought upon their
heads by unthinking, unloving adults. I am glad mine remained
ignorant of much that is polluted, cruel, ugly, hurtful, wrong as
long as possible (which is not, after all, very long, in the scheme of
things) and that their books were wholesome, enriching, enliven-
ing, enjoyable, lovable and, for the most part, were about worlds
into which they could happily, innocently escape.

# Bad Bed-Fellows

... it was unthinkable to put a book by Borges next to one by Garcia Lorca, whom the Argentine author once described as 'a professional Andalusian'. And given the dreadful accusation of plagiarism between the two of them, he could not put something by Shakespeare next to a work by Marlowe, even though this meant not respecting the volume numbers of the sets in his collections. Nor, of course, could he place a book by Martin Amis next to one by Julian Barnes after the two friends had fallen out, or leave Vargas Llosa with Garcia Marquez.

THAT IS FROM a charming novella about the perils and dangers of books and book owning, *The Paper House* by Carlos María Domínguez, which is on a shelf of small books because – well, it is a small book. Before I took it down to copy the quotation, it was sitting next to an old World's Classic edition of *Silas Marner*, but I might replace it beside the *Observer Book of British Moths*, which is also small. I hope they will not quarrel. *The Paper House* is about a man who has many thousands of books which not only take on personalities of their own but come to replace people in his life. A friend went upstairs in his house, 'and as he passed the open bedroom door, on the bed he glimpsed twenty or so books carefully laid out in such a way that they reproduced the mass and outline of a human body'.

So books may drive a man mad. 'Books change people's destinies,' the author writes, and 'Whenever my grandmother saw me reading in bed, she would say, "Stop that! Books are dangerous."'

I go upstairs and downstairs early one February evening when the light is just beginning to fade, looking for something to read and, seeing the shelf after shelf, row after row, pile after pile of pale colours and square shapes, wonder if it is all true. Occasionally, someone is found dead in a house, buried among carrier bags and boxes of things bought compulsively in shops and never so much as opened, or trapped and lost in a maze of piles of old newspapers and magazines. And books. Walled in by books. Immured with books. Killed by books, then. And if one had gone blind and was still inhabiting a house of books? This is indeed the stuff of nightmares. I go downstairs and the books blink at me from the shelves. Or stare. In a trick of the light, a row of them seems to shift very slightly, like a curtain blown by the breeze through an open window. Red is next to blue is next to cream is adjacent to beige. But when I look again, cream is next to green is next to black. A tall book shelters a small book, a huge Folio bullies a cowering line of Quartos. A child's nursery rhyme book does not have the language in which to speak to a Latin dictionary. Chaucer does not know the words in which Henry James communicates but here they are forced to live together, forever speechless. Their covers are closed shut. How can the words breathe? Do the stories only spring to life when we open the volumes out?

Does Elizabeth Bowen find Swift congenial company? Ah yes, surely, they were both Irish, they have a lot in common. I should like to sit here on the landing in the last glimmer of daylight and listen to them whispering together. If I set Richard Dawkins beside the *Oxford Companion to the Old Testament*, will there be the sound of raised voices? I could put a biography of St Francis of Assisi between them to keep the peace, but that would mean tearing St Francis away from a dictionary of animals. Why do we have a dictionary of animals? Where did it come from? Perhaps St Francis brought it with him.

Here is a short run of books about crime, and within crime, principally murder. *Forensic Psychology. The Psychology of the Psychopath. Police Forensics. Crime Scene Investigation. The Female Murderer.* That sort of thing. How much more useful a role they could play if they were moved, en bloc, away from a doorstep encyclopaedia and *Who's Who* (1996) and taken to where they can help solve the mysteries within *Murders in the Rue Morgue, The Moving Toyshop, The Murder at the Vicarage, Devices and Desires, The Journeying Boy, Death of an Expert Witness*. Books should pay rent. On the other hand, they did not ask to come here and they may be unhappy and dissatisfied, bored and prone to put on weight. So perhaps we should pay *them*.

Marlowe, as the man in *The Paper House* well knew, was a drunken, quarrelsome fellow, though we have no reason to suppose that he fell out with Shakespeare. Still, perhaps it is right to keep them apart as we might keep apart Charlotte Brontë's *Jane Eyre* from the novel it inspired, Jean Rhys's *Wide Sargasso Sea*. No. If

Brontë has not yet encountered the Rhys, she should, and she was a woman of sense, open-minded and fair. She would have been interested. Can books learn from one another? Can they change as a result of sitting on a shelf beside another for years? If not, might they regret being forever trapped, as it were, within their own content, doomed never to grow old, never to return to a state before they were created? We find it hard to imagine a world which does not contain us, or at least does not contain knowledge and aware-ness of ourselves even if it does not know our physical presence. We need to know that we are taken account of. When small children put their hands over their eyes they think *you* cannot see *them*.

The last streaks of light have gone from the sky and I am on the upstairs landing in the gloaming. Do the books believe I am no longer there because they do not see me? Can they hear the sound of my breathing? I can still stretch out a hand and grasp one. Does that startle and terrify them, as poor Bill the lizard was terrified when Alice reached down her great hand and plucked him from the smashed roof of the conservatory? Once it is dark and they settle back, do they sleep? Do they move closer together or turn over and re-arrange their covers?

I could take a couple of the picture books for very small children into the drawing room and slip them between a couple of very old books, so old they might crumble to dust if I handle them too roughly – and if books crumble to dust, they die. The books for babies do not know about death nor will they for a hundred years, for their paper is coated and shiny and though pages may become stuck together if the air is damp, they will never crumble away to dust.

Books help to form us. If you cut me open, will you find volume after volume, page after page, the contents of every one I have ever read, somehow transmuted and transformed into me? *Alice in Wonderland. The Magic Faraway Tree. The Hound of the Baskervilles. The Book of Job. Bleak House. Wuthering Heights. The Complete Poems of W.H. Auden. The Tale of Mr Tod. Howards End.* What a strange person I must be. But if the books I have read have helped to form me, then probably nobody else who ever lived has read exactly the same books, all the same books and only the same books, as me. So just as my genes and the soul within me make me uniquely me, so I am the unique sum of the books I have read. I am my literary DNA.

I have put the light on, but the bulb is weak on the top landing. The books have somehow shrunken back into the shelves. Into themselves, like old people hunched into jackets that are too big for them, sleeves that are too long. They seem to be singing.

All through the house, the books are murmuring, turning over in sleep like pebbles on the shoreline as the tide recedes.

But when I reach the stone-flagged hall and stand for a moment, listening, everything falls silent. I hear the comforting, inhabited, friendly silence of a house full of books.

# Sea Interludes

IT BEGAN IN the music room overlooking the garden at my Coventry grammar school. I had done three A levels the previous summer but I had to spend a third year in the sixth form to get Latin, so I kicked my heels, doing double and quadruple Latin lessons, plus odd courses in art and music appreciation. Both of these were a pleasure, more so as they came with neither homework nor exams attached, but the music appreciation was the more interesting because of the enthusiasm and knowledge of one teacher. She introduced us to English composers, for whom she had a passion, talked about their lives and careers, told anecdotes (she herself had studied under Holst) and then played us records. Vaughan Williams, Elgar, Parry, Purcell – wisely, she presented them to us in no particular order so that every lesson was a surprise and if we had not responded to the composer of the previous hour, we might enjoy the one she had for us today. It worked well. I enjoyed the classes.

But one afternoon, something happened to change my life. For some reason, instead of introducing us to the composer, Miss Pellow had decided to play the music first. I can remember everything about the day, as one does remember significant moments. It was the summer term, early May, warm and sunny. The lilac was out in the gardens and the trees had come into the first pale green leaf. Some people were playing on the tennis courts.

And the 'Sea Interludes' from Benjamin Britten's opera *Peter Grimes* came flooding into the music room, with the sunshine. I knew that I was missing the sea. I had been land-bound in the heart of England for two years, after having spent the previous sixteen by the North Sea, and I longed for it every day; but until I heard the music, I had not understood quite how much, nor realised that the sea was in my blood and part of what had formed me and that I would spend the rest of my life longing to go back to it.

I had never heard of Benjamin Britten until that afternoon but the 'Sea Interludes' made me want more of his work and when, on the following afternoon, we listened to Peter Pears singing *Les Illuminations* (some of the poems from which I had studied for A-level French) I knew that I wanted to hear more of that voice, too.

It was the start of a passion for Britten's music, and for the voice of Pears, and of a determination to find out everything about the place on the east coast in which Britten lived and worked and which had helped form him – the same coast, albeit further north, which had helped form me.

Long before I could get to Suffolk something else happened. I continued to discover as much as I could about Britten but at the same time, I had another obsession, one going back to childhood. My maternal grandmother was one of nine children, eight girls and one boy, Sidney, who was killed in the Battle of the Somme. We often went to see my grandmother and there was always a photograph of the beloved young brother, in uniform, on the piano. A new poppy was placed on it every 11 November. I asked a lot of questions about my great-uncle and learned for the first time about the war in which he was killed, alongside so many, many other young men. I read about the Great War and thought about it often. Then, while I was at King's, a friend wrote to tell me she had tickets for the first performance of Benjamin Britten's *War Requiem* in the new Coventry Cathedral, which, she had read, was a setting of poems from the Great War. I walked under the great Euston Arch to catch the steam train home.

The impact of the music, the words, the new Cathedral – the effect of the whole experience is impossible to convey. I had no idea then that both Britten and the Cathedral were to play such an important part in my future life but for the time being, my passion for Britten was consolidated.

He was a composer with a great knowledge and love of literature, and his sound world is steeped in words. For introducing me to so many writers – to Wilfred Owen, Crabbe, Hölderlin, Henry James, and many others, all of whom influenced me profoundly – I owe him the greatest of all debts. Every one led me eventually to write a book of my own, every visit I made to Aldeburgh and Britten-country led me to write more. My obsession with his music, his authors, his places, and especially, at first, with everything to do with the Great War to which I felt such personal ties, continued and became the most important force in my writing life. My links to Coventry Cathedral led to an even more important relationship, out of the anguish of which came another book. But that is a different story.

It was not until 1970 that I managed to get to Aldeburgh at last.

It could not have changed for many years and every inch of it was haunted by Britten and his music. I walked the shingle beach and the steep, narrow streets, I bought a mug in the shop run by Mrs Beech, where Britten had bought a string of them with which to improvise a musical instrument. I watched the lifeboat go out to rescue a fishing boat and saw others sail out every dawn from the beach just below the window of the house I was renting. The music of *Peter Grimes* sang through the sound of the waves rushing up the shingle and every corner spoke of the composer and his life.

By then I had come to know John and Myfanwy Piper. Out of the first few weeks I spent in Aldeburgh in 1970 had come the first book I had written under its spell, a novella called *The Albatross* and, thinking it would be, as they said 'up Ben's street', they sent him a copy. I was terrified of his response but when I went back to Aldeburgh again in 1971, there had been none.

Perhaps I had always known that I would write a book about the First World War but I was afraid of it, uncertain how I could tackle it. For the whole of the preceding winter I had read everything I could lay my hands on – history, militaria, poetry, biography, autobiography, and volumes of privately published letters from young soldiers, produced by their families after they had been killed. And I talked to as many men as I could find who had been in the Great War. There were still plenty of them at that time and I sat listening as they told me variations on the same theme, for the whole of their experience seemed to merge into a single, terrible one. Yet these were men who had lived to fight another day. Slowly, a picture emerged, slowly, characters grew in my mind and in notebooks, until the moment came, not so much when I felt ready to begin as when I could not put off writing the novel any longer.

I drove back to a bitterly cold, sunny Aldeburgh to begin work. And a couple of days after I arrived I received a letter from Britten, telling me how much he had liked *The Albatross* and inviting me to lunch. Every detail of the occasion is carved on my memory. We talked about many things though little about music, partly because it is difficult for a professional to talk about their area of expertise with someone relatively ignorant, however enthusiastic, partly because Britten hated discussing his work at all. He asked what I was writing then and I told him.

'Good luck,' he said. 'I am sure you are right to do it and I quite understand your obsession but I hope you won't be offended if I never read it. I've done with all that and I can't go back to it.'

I did not understand what he meant but I came to do so later, when I had finished the novel. I wrote the First World War out of myself and I, too, have never been able to go back to it.

Because we could not talk about music we talked about books. Ben was well, widely and deeply read – in fiction, in poetry, in biography. He suggested I read two or three Henry James short stories and had the volume numbers of the collected works in which they appeared by heart. If I could not get hold of them he offered to lend me his copies.

I wish I had been able to tell him how much I owed to him but there are never really words for such things.

There are more than thirty books here about him, his life, his letters, his music, his places, and for once they are neatly together on the shelves. I used to re-read them often, now I rarely do. But his influence remains and the greatest debt of any I owe is still to him. Opening a volume of his letters at random, an envelope falls out. It contains a letter from Britten to me. It was in Aldeburgh that I received the telephone call telling me of a death, the call that dealt the heaviest blow of my life. I packed hurriedly and left for home that day, but word reached Ben. His letter was the first I received and the one that gave the greatest comfort, if comfort was ever to be found. He knew how to write it because he had known the man who died and had valued him highly as a musician, because he felt and wanted to express a sympathy that came from his heart, and because he could express himself as well in words as in music.

Looking at the Britten books reminds me of that, as it reminds me of my debt to him, and of the immense privilege of having been touched, personally and professionally, by genius.

But I doubt if he would have wanted me to keep a place for any book about him among my precious forty. He would have urged me to take any of those that had inspired him to write his music, not some volume of musical criticism, account of past Aldeburgh Festivals or collection of his own letters, let alone any biography, which he would have regarded as unnecessary and intrusive.

Crabbe? Wilfred Owen? Henry James? Rimbaud? Hölderlin?

None of those. The Thomas Hardy poems which Britten set as *Winter Words* will fit into a pamphlet, leaving me free to take one of his novels as well.

Besides, we talked about Hardy that bright February day at lunch, discovering a mutual appreciation, and Ben suddenly recited the whole of 'The Journeying Boy' from memory. If I close my eyes, I can see him, sitting in the pale clear east coast light that comes flooding through the windows, and hear the beautiful voice people always remarked on, speaking the lines, plainly and without affectation and so fixing them for ever in my mind.

Hardy it is.

# Hardy

THERE ARE THREE complete editions of his novels here, which is surely two more than necessary, plus some random extra copies lying about. Publishing has always done things the wrong way round, presenting new and untried authors in expensive large-format hardback and then converting them to small, handy, cheaper paperback later. But should authors not earn the right to be printed on better paper, case-bound rather than paperbacked? I know some of Hardy's novels well, and the better I know them and the more I find in them, the more I want to have handsome hardback editions to read. It is as if they had graduated from the cheap, disposable paperback to the format which costs more money and takes up more precious space but which is designed to be kept and treasured. Perhaps the economics of publishing will change things round soon. I know many people who wait for the paperback of a new novel not because they cannot afford to buy the initial hardback, but because they do not want to invest in something so large and apparently permanent when it might be of little merit.

There is a row of paperback Hardy novels here, treated badly, underlined, annotated, dog-eared – or in other words, well read.

I came to many other classic novelists before I had heard of Hardy – Dickens, the Brontës, George Eliot, Jane Austen, Mrs Gaskell … I discovered them myself or was introduced to them in the classroom. When my family left Yorkshire, I was already two terms into the A levels but on arrival at my new grammar school in Coventry, I came up against an entirely different exam syllabus. I had to catch up fast, with Donne and Auden and two different Shakespeare plays, with *Middlemarch* – and with Hardy's *The Return of the Native*. It had already been taught for two terms, so the others knew it well and I had six weeks to get to grips with it for the end-of-year exams. I plunged into the first page and that extraordinarily, and typically Hardyean, opening in which two figures are seen in the distance, crossing the great landscape of Egdon Heath. Wessex was far from the North Yorkshire moors I had left but Hardy's brooding Barrow, his way of writing about places as if they were as important as characters and sometimes more so, was immediately familiar. I responded to *The Return of the Native* at once, so that having to catch up fast, even to the extent of learning the whole opening scene by heart, was a pleasure.

Some people find an author so congenial they can never find fault. I do not know many ardent Jane Austen-ites who are not in love with the entire canon. Perhaps to them she is perfect. But even the greatest authors produce lesser books, as well as books to which the individual reader does not respond. It is certainly true of Hardy. After *The Return of the Native* I picked the next at random, and picked gold with *The Mayor of Casterbridge*, then again with *Far from the Madding Crowd*, but after that, I read *Jude the Obscure* and almost abandoned Hardy for ever. I was saved by *The Trumpet Major* and *The Woodlanders*. Some of the novels can rightly be called great, others are often dubbed minor. *Two on a Tower* or *A Pair of Blue Eyes* are not of the stature of *The Mayor of Casterbridge*, but they are surely not 'minor works' by any reckoning.

And if you want to know and understand Hardy and learn why he is one of the greatest English novelists then reading the lesser-known, but by no means minor, books is essential.

Knowing about a writer's life is rarely necessary to an appreciation of their work. But occasionally it is. I think I understand Dickens better for knowing about his childhood and about his way of working, and I gain more from the Brontë novels by having read a good biography which explained much about their strange, isolated life at Haworth Parsonage (not to mention having gone to Haworth some fifty-five years ago, before it was a commercial trap).

Places tell us so much about certain writers. Although London has now changed out of all recognition, when I first went to live there some of its corners would still have been recognised by Dickens. Though the towns and villages are no longer the same, Hardy's Wessex Barrows and Heaths would be familiar to him. Ten years after first encountering Hardy, in the mid-1960s, I rented a farm cottage in a remote corner of Dorset and drove and walked for miles round the county he knew, where the working country people might have stepped out of his novels. Certainly, they spoke as if they had.

There are some very good biographies of Hardy. I have not re-read the two volumes by Robert Gittings for many years, but he is a sensitive, straightforward, approachable biographer and always rewards a return to his books. So, of course, does the best of all contemporary biographers, Claire Tomalin. Here is her *Thomas Hardy: The Time-Torn Man*, long, exhaustive but clear as crystal. Of how many writers can you say that the life was as interesting as the work? Hardy's was, and so was his melancholic, tormented, personality.

But having read about his anguished affairs and unhappy marriages, his bleak philosophy and pessimistic view of the universe, and man, the tiny inconsequential speck upon its vast impassive face, somehow, it is all made less depressing by Virginia Woolf's account of her one meeting with him, late in his life.

By then, not long before he died, Hardy had become a courteous, slightly vague old man whose novels had been written long before and seemed to mean nothing very much to him. His world had grown smaller, to focus on short walks and his old dog, and though he remembered Virginia's father, Leslie Stephen, and gave them 'what is known as a good tea', he took her book away to sign it and had some difficulty remembering her name before he wrote. She records his wife as being solicitous, as for a child, reminding him gently of this or that, anxious for his health.

It is an altogether touching picture of a younger novelist respectful in the presence of an older and very eminent one, of a man softened and shrunken by age, and above all, one who had come almost to disregard his own genius and what it had produced. Woolf reports that he seemed quite uninterested in his novels. He is never a cold or distant figure, never less than human, but somehow he comes closer to us in this account, and Woolf writes the visit up with great perspicacity and kindness.

Hardy taught me that landscape (and weather) can be as important as character in a novel. He also revealed much about the link between paintings and the novel, and not only in the sense that painters have taken narrative subjects. Scene after scene is illuminated from outside, or from within. When Damon Wildeve and Clym Yeobright play dice by the light of thousands of glow worms on Egdon Heath, the image seems to come straight from one of the Old Masters. Once I noticed the connection, I began to see how often Hardy works like a painter and how, although his narrative line is always direct and clear, he seems to present his story in a series of vivid tableaux. I went to look at some pictures and the pictures led me back to the books. It was probably our excellent English teacher who pointed out the link between Hardy and paintings. I cannot have found it for myself. She was a vague-seeming, nervous woman with a mass of fluffy hair forever escaping from its pins and for a time, until I got the measure of her, I thought she was equally fluffy. But gradually I realised that she taught by releasing tiny droplets of gold from a vial, which you were expected to notice and to catch. The rest was everyday stuff, the plain drinking water of teaching texts clearly and concisely. But it was the golden drops that were stored away, to enrich a lifetime.

After I had left school and was in my final year at university I met her again by chance. She asked what I had been studying, what I liked and did not, what I felt most valuable but when I mentioned my passion for Hardy, she made a wry face. 'I never did much care for Hardy, you know,' she said. It takes a great teacher to teach an author well and to inspire a lasting love for their books, while entirely concealing the fact that they do not much care for them.

# Down among the Women

THIS BOOKCASE CONTAINS 743 books of which 445 are by men. Up a flight of stairs. This bookcase contains 66 books of which 51 are by women. I could go on like this all day and prove nothing except that both men and women write books. But if I pick out only novels, and sub-divide into novels by women, an impressive pile builds up on the floor.

Willa Cather

Carson McCullers

Fay Weldon

Jane Austen

George Eliot

Elizabeth Bowen

Edith Wharton

Margaret Drabble

Olivia Manning

Pamela Hansford Johnson

Isabel Colegate

Emily Brontë

Eudora Welty

Elizabeth Taylor

Charlotte Mendelson

Jeanette Winterson

Anne Brontë

Mary McCarthy

Penelope Mortimer

Penelope Fitzgerald

Virginia Woolf

I might reach 100 women novelists. There are women historians and biographers and other non-fiction authors here too, not to mention the very many women writers of children's books. But again, what does it all prove? What we already know, that writing has always been a strongly female art, whereas women composers and painters are few and far between and that proves – what? That writing can be fitted in most easily between other traditionally female work? Hmm. Jane Austen could hide her novel-in-progress under the blotter if anyone entered the drawing room. The Brontë sisters wrote novels but had to hide their sex behind masculine pen-names. Margaret Drabble could write when her babies were asleep. Most women novelists have had husbands, and therefore another family income. But Vanessa Bell was a painter of great talent and formidable output, who had several children and a busy domestic life, albeit one with servants, whereas Virginia Woolf, her sister, was married but childless. Anita Brookner is single but had a full-time university career. No, whichever way you look at this none of the answers stack up. Perhaps there is no equation at all. A lot of women have written novels. So have a lot of men. Some of them have been good, some bad, some successful, some failures; some women and some men have become rich by writing, others remain poor. If I read a novel which is new to me, without knowing the name of the author, can I tell if it is by a man or a woman? I have never actually tried it. Look at it another way. Here is a copy of *Northanger Abbey*. Could it have been written by a man? Here is *War and Peace*. Could it be by a woman? I think the answer to both is yes, but if I gave you this novel by Trollope how would you guess that it was Joanna and not Anthony – historical context aside? I have written several novels with a male narrator or from a male point of view but a (male) friend who read two of them said he could tell immediately that they were by a woman because they were not obsessed with sex.

For a month I have read only books by women writers, beginning with George Eliot's *Daniel Deronda* which I came to last of all her novels, having begun with *Silas Marner* for O level, and found it dull, though, mercifully, short.

A friend was teaching a first-year undergraduate class on the Victorian novel some years ago, and rather than begin George Eliot with *Middlemarch*, a book she assumed they would all know, she thought she would make life more interesting for them, and asked them to read *Deronda*. None of them had ever heard of it (and indeed, as became clear, none had heard of *Middlemarch* either) so she took a copy down from her shelves. They looked at it in horror. 'What,' asked one, 'you mean read the *whole* of it?' But the whole of it is the whole of a wonderful Victorian novel, an exciting, challenging story full of strong characters – and especially the women, though the villain, Grandcourt, is one of the best depictions of evil I know in fiction. It is the perfect book to discuss, too, full of moral arguments and differing points of view. *Middlemarch* is a flawless book. *Deronda* is not. Some of it is sentimental, some of it tendentious. But it is never less than gripping, and it teems with life and fervour. But might it be by a man? Yes. I think all of George Eliot might be. Might Dickens be by a woman, then? No. But am I saying that because I know and have always known the sex of the authors?

The more I think about it, the more I am sure that that is precisely the case, at least with novels before my own time, except, perhaps, for Jane Austen. Perhaps. *Daniel Deronda* is a book that takes care of a number of cold evenings by the fire. But having finished it, I have glutted on the Victorians. I like reading to be about contrast and change, I like having a jag on crime before turning to essays, being challenged by the sharp angry satire of Swift before relaxing into *The Forsyte Saga*.

But we are still in women-only territory and it is an unusually long time since I re-read Anita Brookner, whose cool, supply written, intelligent novels carry such an emotional charge, a charge well concealed beneath the surface, that always comes as a shock.

Lazy comment often says that Brookner's novels are 'all alike' or 'variations on one theme' in the same way as lazy comment says Jane Austen's novels are narrow and small of focus. Well, Monet painted a series of pictures of haystacks, each one very similar to the last, each adding a dimension to the set, each complementing the other. Bach composed many variations on a single theme. That the argument is a poor one may easily be proved by simply reading every single Brookner novel one after the other, as I have just done. There is a leitmotif running through many of them. The narrator or the principal character is usually a woman, though sometimes a middle-aged man, lonely in some essential sense, usually living in London, sharply self-aware and growing more so, intelligent, perspicacious, often parentally dominated, often without siblings, always middle class, always well educated. The men are interesting though fatally flawed, and their weaknesses are laid bare with a great clarity and understanding, with accuracy but without unkindness. It may seem that the heroines are all alike, all the same woman, but they are not, there are innumerable subtle differences between them, even though they have aspects of a lifestyle in common, and the more you sink into the entire Brookner world, the more you understand what makes for these differences and how subtle but significant they are.

How we repeat our mistakes and why, how we fail to notice vital signs in human behaviour in time to save ourselves from disaster, how we make the best of the bad hand we have been dealt – or how we do not, how we relate to our past and try to make up for it with courage, or give in and blame it for our cowardice, how we betray ourselves more than we betray others, how we make errors of judgement in friendships, in love, how we grow old with or without grace, how we cope with isolation or with poor company – Brookner's novels are about all of these things and more. She is a past mistress at recreating the faded, the sepia, the gloomy, the empty atmosphere, of a hotel, a London mansion flat where daylight barely penetrates the high-ceilinged rooms, a dismal seaside bungalow. She is wonderful on the detail of furniture, clothes, make-up, shopping bought, things cooked and eaten, and she has an uncanny ear for the lame conversations between people who have nothing to say to one another but are yet obliged to talk. She is wonderful on plump, greedy, spiteful, silly, over-made-up women who must pretend still to be young, to flirt and be spoiled as if they were girls, and she knows everything about possessive, selfish mothers, and well-meaning but weak fathers. She is an expert on stoicism, on making the best of it, on bleak self-knowledge and the loss of hope. It is not true that there are no happy endings in her novels but as so often is the case, the happy endings are less convincing, less moving, than the other kind.

The satisfaction and illumination that come from reading more or less nothing but Anita Brookner for three weeks are immense, and have alerted me all over again to how disgraceful it is that so many of her books are no longer in print, how much better she is than talents bruited more loudly abroad, how she ranks among the very best novelists of the late twentieth century.

Could a man have written Brookner's novels? If I had no author's name to guide me, would I be absolutely certain of her sex? In this instance, yes. The insight into the female mind is so acute, so truthful, so sure, that it can only be by one who knows, has experienced, who is not guessing, however cleverly, not playing 'let's pretend'. A man can write with absolute conviction about a woman but not, somehow, do it over and over again without giving the game away.

But as I finish the last Brookner novel and sit by the window looking at the stars prickle in the night sky, turning this question over and over, I know that all I have to go on is instinct, that I could not argue a case convincingly, and that someone somewhere could prove to me that a man might indeed have written these books. In the last resort, does it matter either way?

No. I turn away from the stars and the sliver of bright moon, sure that that is not true either, that it does matter, in some profound sense that is far more than literary. The trouble is that I have not yet worked out what.

I put the Brookner novels tidily back on their shelf – she is a novelist who requires tidiness of her reader, tidiness and attention to detail, application and careful thought. I go to bed, and read the Book of Job, long a favourite. But I am still thinking about why it is that I know a man could not have written the novels of Anita Brookner, whereas one could certainly have written those of, say, Carson McCullers.

Might a woman have written the Book of Job?

# Reading for the Soul

I WAS BROUGHT UP as a Christian, my life has been steeped in Anglicanism, and so I find it unimaginable not to have spiritual reading. There is always something to learn, some wisdom, some new light on eternity, though sometimes what once seemed rich and full of insight and strength does not stay the course.

I remember a conversation with a fellow judge of the then Whitbread Awards some years ago, when the poetry winner was a volume about the death from cancer of the poet's wife, and about his anguish and depth of bereavement in the weeks and months that followed. But within a remarkably short time, he had found a new wife – she even had the same name as the first – and he had brought her with him to the awards ceremony. As a result, my fellow judge said that the book had been completely spoiled for him, and that he could never look on it, or on the author, in the same way again. Was it just a case of the speed of the new love affair and marriage? Would he have felt the same if five or ten years had passed? No, he confessed that he would not. The time lapse made all the difference. He was not being judgemental, simply stating a truth – that the book which had meant so much to him had been fatally diminished for him when he discovered what had happened.

Did I feel the same? Yes, to some extent, though I argued that the poems must stand alone, regardless of the autobiography. But it is something that has gnawed away at me for years. Should it have made a difference? Was our uneasiness justified?

A related question has troubled me about the books by H.A. Williams, which clarified so much, illuminated so many aspects of Christianity, deepened my understanding and supported me through some dark times. Harry Williams knew several close friends of mine, he was a man everyone seemed to love and whose company entertained as well as inspired many. He was Chaplain of Trinity College Cambridge, a gin-drinking, party-loving, socialising sort of priest, as well as one of deep faith. Then he had a severe nervous breakdown which he records in his painfully honest autobiography, *Someday I'll Find You*. After several years of psychoanalysis he retained his equilibrium and out of his turmoil came two remarkable books, *True Wilderness* and *True Resurrection*, which spoke to a great many people at a profound level. Harry took great risks in what he said, he always told the truth as he saw it, he never followed the party line and as a result his sometimes shocking, always brave, sermons and writings drove an arrow straight to the heart of belief and spirituality. As a result of his treatment he not only changed in himself, but changed direction. This affable friend of princes, the aristocracy, the rich and the smart, became a monk in the Community of the Resurrection at Mirfield, in Yorkshire, a move which shocked many, who counselled him that he would be utterly miserable, cut off from the fun-loving life he had been at the heart of, from the theatres, the dinners, the holidays courtesy of well-heeled friends. He knew better. Life in the plain monastic community was his salvation and he recognised it as such. He lived there for many years in a prayerful, supportive community. Illness eventually confined him to his room and he was looked after faithfully, much valued, much loved. But somewhere along the line he lost his faith. He no longer believed in everything he had taught, stood for, fought for, hoped and longed for, and been supported by, all his life. Whether this loss of faith, terrible deprivation, which was akin to losing his life, lasted until his death, I do not know. Once, he would have said that he lost his life to find it. Did he discover the truth of that in the end? I do not know that, either.

But as a result of what I do know, which is simply that he lost his Christian faith, I feel as differently about the books he wrote as a believer as my fellow judge did about the poet who lost his first wife and found another shortly afterwards. It troubles me that I should feel like this and I cannot decide whether I am right. After all, the books have not changed, Harry's beliefs at the time he wrote them were firm and clear. I have not lost my faith. Why should it matter what happened later? Why should it have mattered about the poet and his wives?

More than ever, as I think these things through, I come to the same and only possible conclusion – that the text has to stand alone and the author, their life, and personality before, during and after, are and must remain irrelevant to us, the readers, though, of course, they may be profoundly relevant to the writer. But that is another matter.

My shelf of spiritual reading is not very long because these books need to be read slowly, a few pages, or even just a few paragraphs, at a time. I rely upon these books and come back to them time and again. Michael Mayne's books are so rich on so many fronts that they need to be treated like fruit cake, taken a small, dense slice at a time. He and I first met when he was working for the BBC Religious Affairs department, a job which did not seem the perfect fit. While he was Vicar of Great St Mary's, Cambridge, then Dean of Westminster Abbey, we were not in touch, but after he retired we were briefly on the same committee and our friendship began again – and I started to read his books. We shared a private bond relating to someone who had been important in both our lives, and though we did not share a political viewpoint, and disagreed on one or two other things, it never seemed very important – or not to me.

He was one of the most well and widely read people I have ever known and his deep love and knowledge of literature, poetry, the novel and drama, informed everything he wrote. He took as much spiritual sustenance from art as from the Bible, the Prayer Book and the Anglican liturgy, and reading any of his books opens innumerable magic casements – and is best done with a pen and notebook to hand. Michael's books have always led me to others.

He became famous in a particular way with one book, *A Year Lost and Found*, written after he was seriously ill with a particularly acute and crippling form of ME, while at Great St Mary's. As a result, he became everybody's counsellor and port of call on the subject, which must have been a considerable burden, and I know at least two people who wrote to him in despair during their own bouts of ME and received immediate, generous, thoughtful counsel and advice. You do not have to have the condition to appreciate the book because in a sense it is about any sudden, serious illness which strikes in the middle of a busy life, causing a reassessment of priorities and a change of attitude to many things, not least one's own self. But until his moving final book, he turned away from writing about himself in that directly autobiographical sense – though everything Michael wrote was, to some extent, about himself and his own faith and experience and responses. *This Sunrise of Wonder* is a series of letters to his grandchildren, a kind of bequest of what Ronald Blythe called Michael's 'inventory of joy' – the things in art and nature which, for him, made life supremely worth living and always pointed beyond themselves to God. *Learning to Dance* takes a motif the Elizabethans would have recognised, that life is a dance, or a series of dances, discusses it, plays with it, even, through a series of penetrating readings of books and paintings, music and drama. (He was a passionate theatregoer and for a brief period in early life had thought of becoming an actor.)

I have been taking two pages at a time and going over them line by line, paragraph by paragraph, in that way of reading that St Benedict called *lectio divina*, and which is still used for studying the Bible and the works of the Christian fathers, in monasteries and convents. Many more books than those of the spiritual life lend themselves to *lectio divina* – reading a great novel, and certainly great poetry, in this way is profoundly rewarding and Michael's books, with their many and widely varied references and allusions, their metaphors and wise observations, yield particular riches on slow, concentrated, wholly focused and attentive reading.

His last book is very painful and not to be read lightly or unadvisedly, or indeed very often. He was stricken with a particularly cruel form of cancer of the jaw and underwent aggressive surgery and other treatments, only to have the disease return, untreatable, incurable. *The Enduring Melody* is about this last illness, and it is heart-rending to read but always, through the absolutely clear and honest descriptions, not only of his physical but his mental and psychological state, there is the leitmotif of music, poetry and other writing, which helped to sustain him to the end and which sustains the reader going at least part of the way with him on his bitter journey.

I have gained more from reading Michael's books than from those of any other writer not just about faith and the Christian life, but about all life, any life – and the space they take up on the shelves is holy ground.

There is plenty of theology on my shelves, biblical commentary and other academic work, because, aside from any belief or none, the study is one I have long found interesting from many points of view – historical, cultural, archaeological, geographical, linguistic, metaphorical. It is the same with books about monasticism and in particular the silent orders – the Cistercians, the Carthusians. Paddy Leigh Fermor's *A Time to Keep Silence* and *Halfway to Heaven* by Robin Bruce Lockhart are books to which I turn often. I never come away from either empty-handed. The contrast between the holy silence, calm, peace, order, unhurriedness and deep sense of God of the monastery, and the world outside its walls, always strikes me even when I finish reading a chapter or so of either of these powerful books. Robin Bruce Lockhart spent a week in retreat at St Hugh's Charterhouse, Parkminster, the only English Carthusian monastery, after a serious personal crisis. He was lucky. The monastery does not normally take in guests in this way. His account of what he found there, how it affected him, and of the life of the monks, is profoundly moving and what he felt when he left always strikes home:

On leaving Parkminster that first time, the whole world outside seemed utterly mad. Roads, cars, houses, telegraph poles … all were futile when set alongside the knowledge I now possessed, that within the Charterhouse walls lay eternal truth, eternal wisdom, eternal peace and eternal sanity.

It is a sobering book, not of platitudes, moral precepts, advice, sermonising or preaching, but full of a truth which has been learned, known, experienced, and of God met face to face. It is about the 'peace which the world cannot give' and reading it, like reading the Leigh Fermor, is like drinking draughts of cool water from a deep silent well. There are a couple of dozen more books here on the shelf on the same subject, sitting side by side with the academic theology and biblical criticism, but they never seem right together, any more than the great novels sit comfortably beside literary criticism. They belong to different worlds.

One book of spiritual reading always leads to others – the shelf is constantly refreshed – but I always return to those that have given me most and which continue to bear and yield fruit, year after year. I must put one of Michael Mayne's books – *Learning to Dance*, I think – with *A Time to Keep Silence* and *Halfway to Heaven*, into my forty, because each one is worth far more than the space a single book will take up, each one holds other books within itself, so that in the end, the three become many, many more.

# A Thousand Books
## of the World

SLIPPED RANDOMLY BETWEEN two even more random volumes – the Collins Naturalist *Butterflies* and *The Count of Monte Cristo* is a small red book I do not recognise. Where did it come from?

*The Reader's Guide to Everyman's Library*. It is a nice hardback, beautifully printed, and also on the cover it says 'Working Copy' and 'With the Compliments of J.M. Dent and Sons Ltd'.

I think it must have been given out to bookshops some distant time ago, to help with their ordering, because it is a complete list of all 1000 books in the old Everyman's Library, from its beginning in 1906 to 1956, with an appendix to 1960. It is in alphabetical order, some of the titles have a brief description, and there is the Everyman number printed beside each one. It is a remarkable selection of both well-known classics and the more obscure and long-forgotten, and if you had read, let alone owned, every one of these books, you could count yourself well educated indeed. I wonder if there is anyone alive who has indeed read every one? I have opened it at random, on the letter L, to look for books I have not read, nor even heard of.

Lagerlöf, Selma. (1858–1940) Swedish Author. *Wonderful Adventures of Nils*. 'Illustrated with colour plates and black and white drawings by Hans Baumhauer. This is the Classic Swedish story for children, telling how the boy, Nils Holgersson, became a tiny elf and, riding on the back of a young gander, flew north with a flock of geese and of the exciting adventures they had.'
(There is also *Further Adventures of Nils*.)

Lane, Edward William. (1801–76) English Author and Orientalist. *The Manners and Customs of Modern Egyptians*.

Lever, Charles James. (1806–72) English Novelist. *Harry Lorrequer*.

'Lever was born and educated in Dublin and *Harry Lorrequer*, his first novel, originally appeared in the Dublin University Magazine. A humorous story with a military background, it was an immediate success and the author followed it up with several very popular novels.'

Lyell, Sir Charles (1797–1875) English Geologist. *The Geological Evidence of the Antiquity of Man*.

But also in L are Charles Lamb and La Fontaine, Walter Savage Landor and William Langland, David Herbert Lawrence and Edward Lear, Latimer and Law and Lessing, George Henry Lewes and Abraham Lincoln.

I have this small red book I did not know I owned beside my bed, to open at random if I can't sleep so that I can read about books I have read, books that I have not, books I certainly ought to have read and books I would probably find well-nigh unreadable, and it makes up a fascinating journey through what the compiler of the Everyman's Library thought worthy of being included. I would give a lot to own the complete 1000 books in their original form. The collection would last the rest of my lifetime, and round again, without need to venture further. Reading the brief notes about authors and books makes my mouth water. There is something exciting about so much knowledge and information, so many great works of the imagination, so many stories, all set out here in a volume which is like a cross between a catalogue, a bookshop, a library and an array of samples.

I almost feel that if I could have just one book it ought to be this, because it gives me a taste of a thousand, and that if I read it often enough it will somehow expand, to let out all the other books that are concealed here, concentrated, squashed together rather like the miraculous ZIP files on my computer. I sense that this small red book does actually contain the full texts of every book listed, if only I could find the key to unzipping them. If I did that, they would open out like Japanese water flowers. There may be a concealed spring, or an invisible lock, or perhaps I have to discover the pass-word. However I might get the small red book to yield up its secret and provide me, magically, with the complete library, I will do it. I will not need a lot of shelves, for surely the box can be closed and locked again and everything will be secured tightly inside, like the secret contents of *My Private Diary* with its little brass padlock hanging on the side. Someone could tell me that locked inside the ZIP files of my computer is the text of every one of these books, or that I could purchase a wretched e-reader and download them

– but that is not what I want. I want real books, printed on paper and bound in board and covered in cloth. I know they are in here.

Caesar, Caius Julius. Carlyle, Thomas. Carroll, Lewis. Cellini, Benvenuto. Cervantes, Miguel de. Chaucer, Geoffrey. Chesterfield, Lord. Chesterton, Gilbert Keith. Chrétien de Troyes. Cibber, Colley. Cicero, Marcus Tullius. Cobbett, Coleridge, Collins, Collodi, Conrad, Cook, Cooper, Cowper, Cox, Crofts ...

# Climbing to the Top

AS I CLIMBED to the top of the house I came upon a book here on a stair, another book there on a window ledge, a small pile of books on the step outside a bedroom door, and saw that half of the books here lead a peripatetic life, never knowing where they will be expected to lay their heads next, while the rest sleep soundly for years in the same position, quite undisturbed. But as in the fairy tales, sooner or later someone wakes you, even from a sleep of a hundred years, and so I have woken books and taken them out, shaken them and slapped them on the back, opened them to the light and fresh air, sneezing as the dust has puffed up from their pages. It must have been a shock for them. Or perhaps it was a wonderful liberation, as they were brought back to life and fresh purpose like Lazarus, for a book which is closed and unread is not alive, it is only packed, like a foetus, with potential.

And as I climbed I noticed a paperback half-hanging out of a shelf and found, as I started to push it back, that it was an alphabet book and that it had found its way next to a book of 'Letters and

Lettering', like a child and a grandparent, sitting companionably together. I opened them both and read. Or rather, looked.

A B C D E F G H I J K L M N O P Q R S T U V W X Y Z.

And that is all. True, the alphabet book had coloured letters and beside them pictures of objects. Apple. Bear. Cherry. Dog. And the book had them in lines and repeated patterns, some with curves and curls, some with thick strokes, some with thin, some with flourishes, some plain. Still, it boiled down in the end to just those twenty-six letters. Out of these few marks, plus some small dots and curves of punctuation, every book in this house has grown, every meaning been inserted and extracted, every character created and poem balanced, every lesson taught and learned. All of it packed into and expanding out of twenty-six letters. 'It makes your hair catch fire,' as Charles Causley said.

I have reached the top of the house and the last landing but I have only skimmed the books, there are dozens left alone, unremarked, with the stories that belong to them untold, associations remembered but kept silent.

Here are twenty-three books about Marilyn Monroe, that iconic, extraordinary actress and doomed beauty, exploited, manipulated, destroyed, her story like some terrible fable, her entire life a quest for what she would never find, the happiness and security and love she was never given as a child. Not far away are the plays of her one-time husband, Arthur Miller, and his autobiography *Time Bends*, one of the best modern examples of the genre. I feel I should put them together, for though it seemed an entirely anachronistic and unsuitable marriage, photographs of them reveal it might not have been, that it could have been one of the great marriages – if he had been able to convince her of the fact, and also to wean her from the drugs, legal as well as otherwise, which helped to ruin her. It is, as Ford Madox Ford writes at the beginning of *The Good Soldier*, 'the saddest story I have ever heard'. *The Good Soldier*. I must find it. I must read that again.

I keep pulling out a book and putting it on a window ledge or the floor. I must read this again, and this, and this and that. I must read everything by this author, and that. Arnold Bennett. Mrs Gaskell. Turgenev. Carson McCullers. Steinbeck. Scott Fitzgerald. Evelyn Waugh. Elizabeth Taylor. Joyce Carey. John Fowles. J.G. Farrell. Paul Scott. Thomas Mann. William Golding ... Even Ivy Compton Burnett and Barbara Pym and E.H. Young.

I am taking out far too many books. I need at least another year of reading from home. But now I have reached the landing and here it is. *Howards End*. There is a shaft of sunlight coming through the small window, in which I just fit, so that I can sit on the elm floorboards with my back to the wall.

I open the book.

'One may as well begin with Helen's letters ...'

I read until the sun moves round and I am in shadow again.

# The Final Forty

The Bible
The Book of Common Prayer (1662)
*Our Mutual Friend*. Dickens
*The Mayor of Casterbridge*. Thomas Hardy
*Macbeth*. Shakespeare
*The Ballad of the Sad Café*. Carson McCullers
*A House for Mr Biswas*. V.S. Naipaul
*The Last September*. Elizabeth Bowen
*Middlemarch*. George Eliot
*The Way we Live Now*. Trollope
*The Last Chronicle of Barset*. Trollope
*The Blue Flower*. Penelope Fitzgerald
*To the Lighthouse*. Virginia Woolf
*A Passage to India*. E.M. Forster
*Washington Square*. Henry James
*Troylus and Criseyde*. Chaucer
*The Heart of the Matter*. Graham Greene

*The House of Mirth*. Edith Wharton

*The Rector's Daughter*. F.M. Mayor

*On the Black Hill*. Bruce Chatwin

*The Diary of Francis Kilvert*

*The Mating Season*. P.G. Wodehouse

*Galahad at Blandings*. P.G. Wodehouse

*The Pursuit of Love*. Nancy Mitford

*The Bell*. Iris Murdoch

*The Complete Poems of W.H. Auden*

*The Rattle Bag*. Edited by Seamus Heaney and Ted Hughes

*Learning to Dance*. Michael Mayne

*Flaubert's Parrot*. Julian Barnes

*A Time to Keep Silence*. Patrick Leigh Fermor

*The Big Sleep*. Raymond Chandler

*Family and Friends*. Anita Brookner

*Wuthering Heights*. Emily Brontë

*The Journals of Sir Walter Scott*

*Halfway to Heaven*. Robin Bruce Lockhart

*The Finn Family Moomintroll*. Tove Jansson

*Clayhanger*. Arnold Bennett

*Learning to Dance*. Michael Mayne

*Amongst Women*. John McGahern

*The Four Quartets*. T.S. Eliot